UNDERSTANDING
SPIRITUAL POWER

The *American Society of Missiology Series,* in collaboration with Orbis Books, seeks to publish scholarly works of high merit and wide interest on numerous aspects of Missiology — the study of mission. Able presentations on new and creative approaches to the practice and understanding of mission will receive close attention.

American Society of Missiology Series, No. 22

UNDERSTANDING SPIRITUAL POWER

*A Forgotten Dimension of
Cross-Cultural Mission and Ministry*

Marguerite G. Kraft

Wipf and Stock Publishers
EUGENE, OREGON

Wipf and Stock Publishers
199 West 8th Avenue, Suite 3
Eugene, Oregon 97401

Understanding Spiritual Power
A Forgotten Dimension of Cross-Cultural Mission and Ministry
By Kraft, Marguerite G.
Copyright©1995 Orbis Books
ISBN: 1-59244-309-5
Publication date 8/18/2003
Previously published by Orbis Books, 1995

Contents

Preface to the Series   vii

Preface   ix

PART I
THE PROBLEM

1. Secularizing Christianity   3

2. Spiritual Power and Felt Needs   12

3. Spiritual Power and Worldview   20

4. The Problem with a Western Worldview   31

PART II
THE PERSPECTIVE

5. Theology and the Powers   39

6. Spiritual Power and the Bible   50

PART III
GUIDES AND EXAMPLES

7. Sample Case Studies   67

8. Investigating Supernaturalism   79

9. Modernization and Concepts of Spiritual Power   88

10. Worldview Change in the Case Studies   97

PART IV
STRATEGY

11. Missiological Application   111

12. Conclusion   125

References Cited   133

Index   141

Preface to the Series

The purpose of the American Society of Missiology (ASM) Series is to publish — without regard for disciplinary, national, or denominational boundaries — scholarly works of high quality and wide interest on missiological themes from the entire spectrum of scholarly pursuits relevant to Christian Mission, which is always the focus of books in the Series.

By "mission" is meant the effort to effect passage over the boundary between faith in Jesus Christ and its absence. In this understanding of mission, the basic functions of Christian proclamation, dialogue, witness, service, worship, liberation, and nurture are of special concern. And in that context questions arise, including, How does the transition from one cultural context to another influence the shape and interaction between these dynamic functions, especially in regard to the cultural and religious plurality that comprise the global context of Christian mission?

The promotion of scholarly dialogue among missiologists and among missiologists and scholars in other fields of inquiry may involve the publication of views that some missiologists cannot accept, and with which members of the Editorial Committee do not agree. Manuscripts published in the Series reflect the opinions of their authors and are not understood to represent the position of the American Society of Missiology or of the Editorial Committee. Selection is guided by such criteria as intrinsic worth, readability, and accessibility to a range of interested persons and not merely to experts or specialists.

The ASM Series Editorial Committee
James A. Scherer, Chair
Mary Motte, FMM
Charles Taber

Preface

In working with the Kamwe in Nigeria, the Thai, and the Navajo, I have become convinced that the biblical portrayal of a world filled with spirits is more accurate than that given by Western assumptions. The Bible very clearly presents a world where spiritual powers exist and struggle and tensions between good and evil are in focus. God is clearly a God of power, often revealing himself through "power encounters" with "wicked spiritual forces in the heavenly world, the rulers, authorities, and cosmic powers of this dark age" (Eph. 6:12).

Living in a Nigerian village and, since then, interacting with people from many other societies have made me aware of the variety of ways different peoples interact with these spiritual powers. In order to survive, people in different societies reach out for spiritual power in specific ways according to their worldviews.

The difficulties that drive Christians in many non-Western societies to continue seeking help from pre-Christian power sources have caused me to reflect on God's power and its availability to those who follow him. Investigating the Scriptures, I see a God of power. But Christianity, as carried by emissaries from the West, has left most of the world unable to see God in this way.

This book deals with understanding the dynamics of felt needs for spiritual power in relation to the assumptions, values, and commitments of a people in order to provide a foundation for meaningful Christian witness in spiritual-power–oriented societies. It is my intent to provide a clearer understanding of spiritual-power–oriented societies with the ultimate purpose of introducing a Christianity that allows God to meet all the felt needs for spiritual power that exist in such societies. I show how God worked with similar societies according to the biblical record.

One of my goals is to make the reader aware of the fact that we have received the gospel within a particular cultural perspective. Due to the limitations of that worldview, our understanding and application of Scripture are incomplete. The gospel has been closely tied to our own cultural expression of Christianity and to our interpretations that have arisen as we have read the Scriptures from the perspective of our own worldview and times. The resulting Christianity has usually failed to deal with the active spiritual powers of the environment and the everyday spiritual-power needs of the people.

Urbanization today has brought together people from a wide variety of societies. This book will alert the reader to the place of spiritual power in the lives of such groups as non-Western immigrants, international students, refugees, and businesspeople. Most Christians in the West have little or no understanding of how spirits affect human activity, the power of curses and blessing, the need for harmony with the spiritual forces, and the battles being waged in the spirit world. If we are to share the Christian message and allow Christ to be relevant, we must follow Christ's example and meet receptors where they are. The cultural mix in our own society demands better preparation for Christian witness and church outreach.

The Western Church, under great pressure from rationalism and science-oriented society through the years, has failed to practice a theology of the spirit realm. This has resulted in a lack of awareness of God's power and position in relation to other existing spirit powers. Today there is widespread disillusionment in rationalism and science. In the past nobody would question doctors, medicines, engineers, science, or education. Today all are being challenged. Humans have not come up with all the answers that were promised for successful living. Now many Westerners are turning to variations of Eastern religions and seeking spiritual-power assistance through New Age and other related groups. It is my hope that the material presented in this book will give greater meaning to the power of the Holy Spirit within Christianity and the way this relates to life in today's world.

My study focused on spiritual power in Scripture and specific anthropological research done on the role of spiritual power in three different societies: Thai, Navajo, and Kamwe. The results of the study showed that common felt needs drive people in these societies to seek spiritual power. I deal with the modernization process and how it affects spiritual-power concepts in these three societies. The potential receptors of the gospel are already relating to specific spiritual powers in a prescribed way to meet their felt need for power. By understanding the basic assumptions and values in these societies, one can see how the gospel must be translated into forms they can understand, allowing it to encompass all areas of life. These case studies provide a model that can be used in other mission contexts.

In many societies of the world several areas of life are considered "spiritual" that are not so considered in the West. These worldview differences often result in spiritual-power needs being overlooked by the church. I have suggested specific strategies for more effective communication of the gospel in spiritual-power–oriented societies. I have shown how the receptor's worldview affects how the gospel should be presented, how the message is heard, the response itself, and the establishment of the church.

I am deeply grateful to the late Dr. Alan R. Tippett, who supervised the doctoral study on which this book is based, and Dr. Paul G. Hiebert and Dr. Arthur Glasser, who also provided valuable teaching and guidance. I especially thank the members of the Thai, Navajo, and Kamwe societies who provided information that made this book possible. I am grateful for the encouragement and assistance I have received from Biola University. My colleagues have been supportive and patient, and Biola University awarded me a Faculty Research Grant that assisted me in the field research. My special thanks and appreciation go to my husband, Dr. Charles H. Kraft, whose patience, faithful prayers, and encouragement have made this book possible. I also offer praise to God for tapping me on the shoulder and challenging me to make this contribution to his work. It is my prayer that this will be used in furthering the work of his kingdom on this earth.

PART I

THE PROBLEM

Chapter 1

Secularizing Christianity

Patra, who lives in Thailand, became a Christian three years ago, but her entire family is Buddhist. When her daughter Huai became very ill with a high fever, Patra took her to the hospital even though the relatives felt she should go to the spirit doctor. The fever continued. When she was not able to get help at the hospital, she brought Huai home. Patra then took her daughter to the spirit doctor, who explained that an evil spirit from a woman who died in childbirth was taking children's lives. Patra was instructed by the doctor to prepare an offering for the spirit, and when she did the child's fever went down immediately and she was well.

Bubwa, a farmer in Nigeria who became a Christian while attending the mission school as a boy, joined in an agricultural program sponsored by the church. He learned that productivity of the farm is related to the richness of the soil. The agriculturalist instructed the students in the use of fertilizer to build up the soil. Bubwa followed the teaching faithfully, but for two years his crops were not good. In desperation he went to the local diviner to find out what was the problem. He was told that his crops were failing because he had offended his uncle. He must go speak with him, settle their differences, and participate in a traditional forgiveness ceremony. Bubwa did as instructed, and the next year his farm produced bountifully.

Taiko, a leader of the women's group in a Micronesian Christian church, became very distraught when she heard that her brother was preparing to sell some of the family land in order to buy himself a new boat. Since the land is owned communally by the woman's clan, Taiko stood to lose. She talked to her pastor, who said he would pray. As the time for the completion of the transaction drew closer, she felt that she must contact the *itang*, the specialist in tribal lore who has special insight and power from the clan spirit. Since women are perceived as impure due to menstruation, she arranged for a family male mediator to approach the *itang*, who then used spiritual power to stop the sale of the land.

Christianity and the West have brought to the non-Western world many new ways of doing things, but often there have been disappointment and frustration as well. Christians have tried to follow biblical teaching and Christian ideals, but often they have come up short on answers for the impending dangers of life. Or at times the Western treatment/answer simply does not work because it does not deal with the problem as the non-Westerners perceive it. Modern technology, Western education, and new religious forms have often failed to deal with the spirit world and its involvement in daily living.

The story of Pete Greyeyes, a Navajo medicine man, illustrates how God met Pete on his own turf and how God's power protected him from witchcraft and the resulting illness:

> One day his body began breaking out in sores, while at the same time up to a score of owls began gathering in the juniper trees outside. The owls, he "knew" represented his ancestors coming to warn of sickness, calamity or even death. Pete administered the antidote, which was to have another medicine man come and "sing" over him. One was called, and then another. Pete even used his own medicine pouch and prayer songs, but to no avail.
>
> When Pete's wife and daughter also broke out with sores, they became desperate and together decided to go to Herman Williams, a Navajo preacher. They arrived at his church service one night just as Herman was concluding the invitation. Pastor Williams was startled to see this medicine man come forward with his family and ask for prayer. After the service, the pastor brought the family to his home where he prayed for them and told them about Christ into the early hours of the morning. Late that night, the whole family turned to Christ. As the family was about to leave around 3 a.m., Pete suddenly remembered the owls. "How will Jesus get rid of them?" he asked. Pondering for a minute, the pastor finally said, "When you get home tonight I want you to go out under those trees and preach to the owls in the name of Jesus Christ." On the pickup ride home Pete tried to dismiss the idea. He understood witchcraft, but he wasn't crazy! His wife had taken the advice seriously however, and would not let Pete into the hogan until he "preached to the owls." So he went under the juniper trees and talked directly to the owls. "There is no reason," he began with some hesitation, "for any of you to stay here because we belong to Jesus now. I belong to Jesus, my family belongs to Jesus, our hogan belongs to Jesus, our sheep, cows, and horses belong to Jesus; our pickup belongs to Jesus; and everything you see here belongs to Jesus. There is no reason for you owls to stay. You can leave now."
>
> Feeling somehow relieved, Pete went into his hogan and fell sound asleep. In the morning the owls were gone and never returned. The

sores of all members of the family quickly healed. Jesus was their new master. (Scates 1981:3–4)

Pete's experience in this power encounter showed him clearly that his medicine bag was powerless to help him when he really needed it and there is greater power in Jesus Christ.

Lesslie Newbigin has pointed out that Christianity is the most secularizing force in recent history (1966:18). The reason behind this is that a form of Christianity that is comfortable in the West has been transferred to other parts of the world. It fails, however, to deal with the whole person as an integrated spiritual being. The categorizing of life, as in the West, influences the establishment of institutions to provide for various areas of life: church for the religious area, schools for the educational area, hospitals for the physical/medical area, organizations promoting agricultural technology for the economic area, and groups promoting developmental technology for the production and health area. Much of the world experiences supernaturalism as the center and integrating force of life. In these societies there is a primary concern with spirits and the spiritual realm. Without this central focus the impact of such foreign emphases is "secular."

The type of Christianity visible in Europe and America today lacks integration. It is very easy and common to see little or no relationship between faith in God and business ventures, quality of work on the job, use of leisure time, or interaction with family and friends. The spiritual is usually seen as an area of life that needs to be tended to, but all other areas of life are separate from it and to be controlled by the individual. Dallas Willard, in his practical book on how to live as Christ lived, evaluates the state of the American church today, showing how Christianity has slipped from what was intended by God according to Scripture:

The American church has overestimated the good that comes from mere scientific progress or doctrinal correctness, or from social progress, missionary work, and evangelism. The church has been shaken to its foundations by ideological, technological, and military movements on a scale never before experienced by humankind, as it has been smothered by mass culture, mindless "prosperity," insipid education, and pseudo-egalitarianism. And as a result, the church at present has lost any realistic and specific sense of what it means for the individual believer to "grow in the grace and knowledge of our Lord and Savior Jesus Christ," as 2 Peter 3:18 expresses it. In fact, it has lost sight of the type of life in which such growth would be a realistic and predictable possibility. (1988:16)

He then describes the main disciplines for spiritual life with Christ as the model for living. This allows Christ to be a part of all areas of life and to be the integrating force. The cultural segmentation of life for Americans makes this a very difficult process.

Most missions have established schools, hospitals and clinics, publishing houses, agricultural programs, and/or veterinarian programs along with establishing the church. These institutions were set up according to Western patterns and unconsciously promoted Western values. Foreign values include among others these concepts: wealth is in material goods more than in strong family ties; spiritual things can be taken care of on Sunday and Wednesday nights; the individual is more important than the welfare of the entire family; monogamy is right, polygamy is wrong; competition is the way to get ahead; women should have freedom with opportunity to do whatever kind of work they choose; time is limited and tasks must be done "efficiently" (including not "wasting time" with people). Secularization and Western values have been a part of the worldwide Christian movement.

At the same time it has not been important to the missionaries to learn about the way things have been done traditionally so that the institutions might adapt to the situation. For many years foreign missionaries and development programs did not allow the local people to be involved in policy/decision making. This resulted in the institutions being foreign in structure and geared to meeting foreign needs, not the needs perceived by the local persons. Christianity has been the carrier of many scientific developments to the Third World. No one would question the value of providing literacy, schools, hospital care, medicines, and other results of scientific discovery, if the local people are ready and interested. However, we must be ready to adjust the foreign system to fit the local situation and to tend to problems that result when these new things are incorporated in the society. For instance, hospitals may need to shift their emphasis to preventive care — teaching nutrition and health care at home — in order that in the long run they can be more effective when treating patients within the hospitals themselves. Schools, by taking children away from home and failing to emphasize respect for parents and traditional values, have often participated in the lowering of moral standards for the society and thus added many new problems, for example, pregnancy before marriage, abortions, and early deaths.

WHAT IS THE PROBLEM?

When a Western approach to life is brought to a non-Western land, a serious cross-cultural problem often results. As the Westernization process takes place there is change from a more traditional way of life to a more complex, technologically advanced, and rapidly changing style of life. Competition replaces cooperation, efficiency replaces participation, outside products replace artistic personal expression, and striving to survive replaces gratification. A wide cultural gap exists between societies that have different basic assumptions and values. I will deal with several specific areas where the Western approach to life differs from the traditional approach.

1. Institutions, following Western patterns, do not take a holistic approach but rather tend to be concerned only with how well the job is being done. When persons fail to produce efficiently, they are let go, whether or not they need the job. Too little attention is given to what happens to the whole person. The fragmentation of life makes it difficult to feel self-value and fulfillment. If the traditional approach was being followed, jobs would be created in order to keep the employees, or arrangements would be made for someone else to hire them. God's intention is that we be holistic, as Christ demonstrated for us in his life. With this priority it may be necessary to slow down the amount of scientific change in order to be sure areas of greater value are dealt with, for example, self-image, spiritual power, family relations, and independence from foreign control. Working with the whole person means focusing more on people than on programs, and this is not the usual American way.

2. Institutions and modernization create an impersonal idiom. As public and private life become separated, there is a search for identity. When following the traditional approach, one meets the same person in many different social situations, so there is a better chance of knowing the whole person. With the Western approach, one sees certain people only at work, others only at home, others only in the store, others only at church, others only at school, and so on.

The Western approach to life has a dehumanizing effect. A person is only valued for services rendered and then paid on a time basis. In the production of goods, time and quantity are more important than the quality of the finished product. More often than not there is no personal relationship with the employer, so there is very little affirmation for the work done. Furthermore, there is little personal satisfaction in doing the work, so the focus is placed more on the money earned.

In native Alaska, some of the problems in the modernization process have been recognized. Norman Chance gives the following helpful suggestions for being sure that such changes do not dehumanize:

A truly modernizing Alaska is one in which native and non-native Alaskans engage together in transformation designed to denounce technological and social changes that dehumanize in favor of a more balanced approach to social development that "announces" the creative humanizing qualities presently submerged in a culture of silence. (1974:352)

The "culture of silence" as the author uses it here refers to those who have no consciousness of self except in a dependent relationship to those in a more dominant economic, social, and political position.

Because Christianity is involved in the modernization process, Christians must guard against the possibility of having a dehumanizing effect on society. Knowing that foreign institutions promote this through impersonalness and a focus on getting the job done, it is important to constantly be aware of the fact that God made all human beings to be creative, to be decision makers, and to be responsible for their actions. The church can reinforce this by cooperation, participation, and providing opportunity for creative expression from within the society. It may be necessary to denounce or slow down changes that do not build up the whole person.

3. The Western approach to life also differs greatly from the traditional in the area of the importance of spiritual power. For the Westerner, faith in and commitment to science give humans control over the material universe.

Western societies passed through the Renaissance, the Reformation, the Enlightenment, and a wide variety of ripples and spin-offs from these movements.... The result: God and the church were dethroned, and the human mind came to be seen as savior. It is ignorance, not Satan we are to fight. And our weapons are human minds and technology. God, if there be a God, only helps those who do it all themselves. Thus, by the nineteenth century, God had become irrelevant to most Westerners. (C. Kraft 1989:31–32)

Christians, then, in the West struggle to combine a secular worldview and the God of the Bible. Spiritual powers and their place in the universe are given very little attention or relevance in daily living.

It is interesting to notice that modernization in American society has not brought satisfaction to many. For years now we have been taught that science has the answers. However, openness to the New Age movement and Eastern religions, which are gaining popularity in our society, is an indication that even Americans are seeing a spiritual side of being human that needs attention. Perhaps if we can envision a faith that permeates all areas of life — social, economic, political, educational, business — plus a faith that can meet the issues of the day head-on so it does not get outdated, we will be able to work more effectively within a modernizing world.

In contrast, for many non-Western societies the spiritual realm is the center of life. Humans are seen as weak and needing increased strength to survive in a world full of spirit activity. To illustrate, the Bantu see themselves in intimate and personal relationship with nonhuman forces:

> *Force*, the *potent life, vital energy* are the object of prayers and invo-
> cations to God, to the spirits, and to the dead, as well as of all that is
> usually called magic, sorcery, or magical remedies. The Bantu will tell
> you that they go to the diviner to learn the words of life, so that he can
> teach them the way of making life stronger. (Tempels 1945:31)

According to the Bantu's worldview assumptions, all that happens in life is related to vital force. Each society has its own way of obtaining spiritual power for times and events that are filled with unknown dangers and for situations that are beyond human control.

Ideally, in societies where supernaturalism is the center of life already, great care needs to be taken to avoid secularization. The person of Christ becomes the center when one becomes Christian. Just as spiritual power was necessary for success, wealth, guidance, and meeting daily crises (for example, illness, accidents, barrenness, and drought), so Christ will need to be involved in each of these. For the Western missionary it will be difficult to teach, practice, and model this integrated life rather than the "secular" presentation of medicine, human accomplishments, totally scientific explanations, and self-reliance. God's part in a successful agricultural project, physical healing, interpersonal relationships, protection from dangers, finding a job, and personal achievements will need to be kept in focus. Dependence on spiritual powers in pre-Christian experience makes it much easier to depend on God as a Christian.

The deep-rooted belief in spiritual powers that are active in daily life changes much more slowly than other elements of culture. Philip Hughes, while doing his Ph.D. dissertation, researched Buddhist and Christian Thai beliefs and values. Responses to his questionnaire indicated that becoming a Christian did not change one's conceptual categories or most of one's presuppositions (1982:231). Hughes writes:

> The results of the questionnaire gave little evidence that there has
> emerged a Christian subculture which has different terminal values,
> concerns, or concepts of evil from the larger Buddhist culture. Indeed,
> cultural non-religious factors appear to be much more significant than
> differences in religious affiliation itself in affecting beliefs and values
> in these areas. (Hughes 1982:158)

As many Christians as Buddhists indicated that the spirits could be causes of such problems as road accidents and sickness. This shows

that the spirits are just as much a part of the world for the Christian
students as for the Buddhist students. (1982:184)

Christians should not supplicate the spirits, however, but be taught to claim
the power of Jesus over them. This illustrates how when people accept
Christ, Western worldview assumptions do not replace the local worldview
assumptions, but rather the configuration changes.

My own experience living in a Nigerian village and since then interacting
with people from many other countries has caused me to reflect on the variety of ways different groups interact with spiritual powers of various kinds.
Questions have arisen in my mind. Should all Christians have the same concept of God? What has God already revealed of himself to those in other
societies? How does God respond to other spiritual powers that are so real
to those in other societies? How can the God of Scripture be the God of
power for the everyday lives of Christians in a spiritual-power–oriented society? These questions along with many others have driven me to investigate
both cultures as designs for living and the Scriptures as God's message for
humankind.

There are other questions I hear coming from the minds and hearts of
Christians or potential Christians from other societies. Does the foreign doctor know how to take care of the spirits who are making me ill? How will I
know when to plant my crops if I do not go to the diviner? Does the pastor
have enough spiritual power to deal with my wife's barrenness? What will
happen to me when I die if I am not buried with the clan members? What
can I do to keep my husband from taking the second wife for whom the arrangements are being made? How can I survive the curses of my father when
he hears of my Christian faith? Where within the church is there power to
protect me from witches? In fact, when discussing Christianity with a non-
believer from another society, the question raised is often not, Who is this
Jesus? but What can Jesus do?

This is a book about spiritual power — suprahuman power. This nonhuman power is regularly sought by humans in time of need. Often people
of the West seek this power only when backed into a corner, for example,
when someone has an incurable disease or when one is taken captive and is
helpless. Most of life is seen as being under human control. In most societies
of the world, however, people see themselves as needing spiritual assistance
each day. I have chosen not to use the term "supernatural" to avoid the dualism implied by the term. Many societies do not see a clear division between
natural and supernatural or would see that division differently than Westerners. This will be discussed more fully later in the book. The purpose of this
book is to show that (1) basic human needs cause individuals to reach out for
spiritual power and (2) worldview assumptions and values program human

interactions with spiritual powers. A meaningful cross-cultural Christian witness and the development of a relevant church require an investigation of pre-Christian beliefs and practices in order to be in touch with peoples' spiritual-power needs.

Chapter 2

Spiritual Power and Felt Needs

A few years ago a Navajo Christian acquaintance was speaking to my class about Native American life experiences. He told of his move from the reservation to the city, the difficulties — even living on Skid Row. He joyfully spoke of his faith in Christ and his faithful family who helped rescue him from the streets. But he said as he tried to interest other Navajo in following Christ they were uninterested, saying, "There is no power in Christianity. We need power to survive in this world." He was aware of the Navajo worldview with lots of spirit activity, and he had not been taught how to handle this as a Christian. This is just one example of the powerless Christianity that is experienced in so many parts of the world today.

The Navajo have a holistic approach to life, and the concept of harmony is the central focus. They believe that everything was brought into being in perfect harmony — a balance between human beings and the world around them, between human beings and the spiritual powers around them. Unity in the spirit realm generates a feeling of understanding, concern, peace, and identity with the surroundings — in nature, people, animals. When disharmony arises (for example, sickness, misfortune, strained relationships, breaking of a taboo, contamination from outsiders), harmony must be restored. To do this it is necessary both to diffuse evil powers and to bring good powers. Disease and injury are often of spiritual origin, caused by witchcraft, sorcery, or contact with ghosts. "Positive health for the Navajo involves a proper relationship to everything in one's environment, not just the correct functioning of one's physiology" (Witherspoon 1977:24). Because of this belief the traditional and Peyote ceremonies deal with the whole person, his/her family, clan, animals, fields, origins, and the spirit powers around the person. For Christianity to meet the felt needs of the Navajo there must be a greater understanding of the Navajo universe and also some restructuring of the Western-style church and its activities.

In the study of individuals and societies through the years there has been an awareness of felt needs, which some have referred to as "wants" or "desires." These are recognized needs, sometimes consciously and other times unconsciously recognized. These felt needs include the need for food, shelter, protection, identity, communication, belonging, and security. Basic felt needs can be grouped into four areas: biological, social, spiritual, and psychological. They are common to all human beings. Basic needs have been described and categorized in a variety of ways by a number of psychologists and anthropologists (Barnett 1953; Maslow 1970:53; Herskovits 1951; Linton 1952:646).

Basic needs are shaped by cultural values and programming. They are also influenced by the environment. For instance, in various parts of the world the need for shelter could be satisfied by an ice house, a group of grass-roofed huts, a tent, a cardboard lean-to, a log cabin, a three-bedroom house, or a mansion. The felt need for safety might be satisfied by being surrounded by family (relatives), having a watchdog, hiring a security guard or a body guard, installing bars on windows and locks on doors, or living in a friendly neighborhood. The manner in which the needs are met is affected by societal and personal values and the available resources. Often meeting needs moves from the survival level to an elaboration level. Food needed to survive is one thing; the food on many tables in the United States is quite another thing and well illustrates the elaboration level.

Felt needs are the source of motivation to action. To illustrate, the need for wealth motivates some to work hard, others to steal, others to make things right with spiritual powers, others to have large families. In one society the belief is that if you work hard you will be rich. In another group the belief is that you deserve more than you have, so you can take from others to get your due. In another society you do not get rich without the gods making it so with their blessing. Still another society defines wealth as the extended family, so the larger the family, the wealthier you are. Felt needs motivate, but the societal beliefs and values shape the resultant action.

Bronislaw Malinowski, one of the first professional anthropologists to base his analysis on his own fieldwork, was interested in what human needs are fulfilled by cultural patterns. He felt that religion was born out of the tragedies of life, out of the conflict between human plans and the realities of life. He pinpoints people's desire for immortality and their craving for communion with God as "twin needs which we all feel, which man has felt from the beginning, whenever he has been unable to face his destiny" (1931:75).

There is a great variety of physical, psychological, and social needs that are common to all humans. However, the common felt needs relevant to the purpose of this book are those that relate to spiritual power. Human beings seem to know they have limitations and seek help beyond their own capabilities. Each society has its own way of obtaining spiritual power for times and events that are filled with unknown dangers and for situations that are beyond human control. In many societies of the world the quest for spiritual power for daily living is at the forefront of the people's minds. I use the term "spiritual-power–oriented" to describe such societies.

Seeking after spiritual power in Africa has been described by D. Westermann:

> This craving for power is the driving force in the life of African religion....Man is weak, and what he needs is increased strength.... The absorbing question for him is how to acquire some of this power so that it may serve for his own salvation or that of the group for which he is responsible. (1937:84)

The need for the spiritual to enable human beings — who are perceived as weak and limited — to survive each day is real in many parts of the world today.

Edwin W. Smith, writing on African ideas of God, speaks of the individual needs for spiritual power and the way many of these needs are satisfied:

> Amulets and talismans, vehicles of metaphysical energy, provide protection and good fortune in many directions and produce confidence in times of crisis. [The African's] confidence can never, however, be complete, for he never knows whether some malicious person will not get possession of more potent "medicines" than his. (1950:29)

By the use of charms and spells, on the one hand, and sacrifices and prayers to spirit powers, on the other, one is able to preserve one's life. Life is a very serious struggle between spiritual powers, and humans must deal with them carefully.

In my research of concepts of spiritual power, I investigated three different societies: the Navajo on the reservation, the Thai in Thailand, and the Kamwe in Nigeria (M. Kraft 1990). I asked people why they sought spiritual power. The overlap in their responses led me to look for the basic human needs that are common to all three societies. I also investigated ceremonies and religious practices that relate directly to specific felt needs for spiritual power of either individuals or groups within the society. I grouped these needs in six categories: (1) perpetuity needs, (2) prosperity needs, (3) health needs, (4) security needs, (5) restitution needs, and (6) power needs.

1. *Perpetuity Needs.* This group is constituted by the felt needs that are related to maintaining the lineage, tribe, and people. A very common reason people seek spiritual assistance is barrenness. The family depends on reproduction to maintain itself and the people. If reproduction in one

family fails, difficulties arise in many quarters. Adults depend on off-spring for personal care in their old age, and tribes and villages depend on the young for strength. The poorest of the poor is the person without a family.

To ensure fertility, spiritual resources are employed in many societies. Ancestors and other specific spirits or gods are contacted to guide in the choice of marriage partners and to provide offspring. A barren woman goes from one source of spiritual power to another seeking power sufficient to give her a child. People seek spiritual assistance, too, when problems arise in a marriage. Women purchase love charms to hold their husbands or seek out spiritual-power practitioners to place a curse on the woman who is interfering in the marriage.

Fertility also relates to land, crops, and livestock. The Kamwe, a horti-cultural society, recognize that in order to have a good crop spiritual power is necessary. A special community ceremony is held to seek God's help and blessing on the people's work at both planting time and harvest time. For the Navajo, a pastoral society, sheep are seen not only as wealth but as a measure of family well-being. The male Navajo's link to his herds involves deep emotional ties — his family's continuity and well-being and his own self-image are symbolized by his herds. Ritual songs regularly call for good health and fine healthy animals.

2. *Prosperity Needs.* Many people believe they need spiritual help to prosper and move through life in an orderly progression. Transitions are often marked by rites designed to draw on spiritual powers to assist in child-birth, puberty, marriage, and death. Initiation into a new status in life usually involves seeking special help from a spiritual power.

An important spiritual power to the Thai is the soul-spirit that lives within each individual. It is involved mostly with prosperity, good health, and orderly progression in life. It is thought to wander from the body, so every life-cycle move requires a soul-tying ceremony to be sure to keep this spirit in the body during the transition.

Building a house may require special spiritual preparation and blessing. Many times when a decision has to be made, it is comforting, and sometimes even essential, to get advice from a spiritual source. In Thailand, monks, knowing the auspicious times of spiritual power, often through astrology, are called on to set the date/time for special occasions, for example, opening a new business, marriage, a funeral, or choosing the place for a new spirit house.

A person or group's helplessness in the face of death often drives them to interact with spiritual powers in an elaborate ceremony. Death for the Kamwe is a time when the family all return home and the dead person is honored. Burial rites are important because the spirit must get off to a good start in the spirit world. Traditionally the length of the funeral (the number of days) is an expression of the importance of the person who has died. The corpse is honored as it is propped up to be a part of the crying and dancing. The extended celebration allows the family and community to adjust gradually to life without the person who died. The people left are then to remember the ancestors in every important event that takes place within the family.

3. *Health Needs.* Sickness and treatment of illness are often tied to spiritual resources in some way. The linkage varies according to a society's theory of sickness. In some, sickness is thought to be caused by neglecting an ancestor or other spiritual being or by breaking a taboo. In others, it involves human causes, such as sorcery or witchcraft. In all of these, spiritual powers must be dealt with. Even if the sickness is attributed to natural causes, the treatment may involve spiritual powers. Accidents, too, may be explained in spiritual terms, requiring spiritual remedies.

In Thai society illness is often perceived as having a spiritual cause. Two of the persons I interviewed explained how they were taken to the hospital very ill, and nothing could be done to make them well; after they returned home, the spirit doctor was contacted, and by following his instructions they got well immediately.

Sulamith Heins Potter related the incident of a man who sent his children to cut down a tree he had purchased for firewood. The son, Keen, climbed the tree and did the cutting. He was struck that night with a paralyzing illness and could not even speak. After a day and a night with no signs of recovery, the father sent for a spirit doctor:

> They sent for a man named Father Eye, whom they liked and respected, and who has the spiritual strength to deal with supernaturally caused illnesses. Father Eye listened to their story, and then he said that Keen was being attacked by the spirit which had inhabited the tree. He thought that the spirit could probably be appeased by an offering of chicken and rice wine. Father Good got some rice wine and a chicken, and taking Father Eye with him, went to the place where the tree had been. They built a little platform as a sort of altar and offered up the chicken and the rice wine. Soon after they returned home, Keen began to recover and by the next day he was quite well. (1977:119–20)

Offending a spirit may at times be an unconscious act, and the spirits usually will accept an offering and an apology.

4. *Security Needs.* Another kind of felt need is the need to feel secure. This may involve taking precautions to contact spiritual sources before going into an unknown territory or undergoing purification when one returns.

Natural disasters such as drought and floods often cause people to approach spiritual powers for help. These dangers require protection from evil and misfortune. The same is true of accidents. Similarly, when things are lost or have been stolen, a person may seek spiritual assistance in locating them.

When there is drought, the Kamwe traditionally reach out to God for assistance. The whole community feasts and makes a sacrifice; then the young people and adults go up the mountain to dance. The mountain is seen as a place that is closer to God. The tradesmen musicians beat the drums and play other instruments. This is the way the Kamwe attract God's attention to their need and also the way they bring pleasure to God.

Among the Navajo, the sorcerer uses imitative magic with something from the victim (for example, clothing, hair, fingernails) and recites a spell to accomplish his purposes. Each sorcerer claims to be assisted by a spiritual power. One of the people I interviewed had been called on to help when a Navajo girl was found on the ground in a comatose state. Her family had found a piece of cloth in the back of their pickup truck with the family's picture wrapped in it and with lightning marks on it. For the Navajo lightning is always an evil power. Previously the girl's family had had a car wreck, and later another family member had been rushed to the hospital. The family was convinced that all of this was caused by an evil power. It needed to be dealt with on the spiritual level.

5. *Restitution Needs.* A concept of right and wrong behavior is a part of all societies. Each has prescribed ways to restore order after someone has broken the rules. Often breaking the rules of society is seen as offending the ancestors. In this case a ceremonial offering must be made to them. For the Thai the ancestors are the guardians of traditions as a moral way of life. A special shelf is constructed in the house, and offerings according to what pleases them are placed on it regularly by the leaders of the family. When the ancestor spirits are offended — for example, when a member of the family breaks physical contact rules while courting — a specific food offering is required.

Spiritual power is often used to restore relationships. Purification and forgiveness often require a ritual performed before a spiritual power. Restitution may require a sacrifice or an offering to a particular spirit. Purification rites may also be needed before contacting that spirit power.

The Kamwe have a special ceremony called *tsahwi* that is used in restitution. The literal meaning of the word is "take it out of the stomach" or "spit it from the stomach." This ritual is performed when the family is not at peace with one another or when things are not going well, when there are strained relationships. Each person takes a few grains of guinea corn, puts them in his/her mouth, chews them, spits them on the ground, and recites a ritual statement that all bad things in the stomach-heart are to be gone through

God's blessing. The finality of the restitution is stressed. This ritual is often used effectively when forgiveness is needed.

6. *Power Needs.* Most human beings have a sense of limited power and a consciousness that more power exists beyond them, namely, spiritual power. They believe this power is available for humans to meet their felt needs. People in every culture face events that they cannot explain and things they cannot control. Many things in life can be handled by humans, but then there are areas where each person feels limitations. In some societies to fish close to shore does not require spiritual power, but to fish out in the deep, persons must seek spiritual protection by performing a ritual before they go. Human technology suffices in many areas of life, but there are areas in life where people have no control.

When the Thai travel outside of their home area, they need spiritual power for protection from the unfamiliar spirits around them. For this they use amulets, often one or more Buddha images. They live in a universe where there are a great number of autonomous spirits with which a person must learn to interact. Guardian spirits, each with its own territory, are benevolent if cared for but may act malevolently if offended or ignored. Humans in an area establish a spirit house where the spirit lives and is cared for. Traveling in Thailand, one sees spirit houses in many locations: in the yard of a home, at hotels, at businesses, at universities, in fields, on village property, along the road where accidents have happened. These spirits want and need to be respected and supplicated for ensuring the welfare of human beings on their turf, but they have no influence or power outside their own borders.

I am aware that some of the specific needs requiring spiritual assistance may fit in more than one category. For example, in Thai society a person places a gift at the spirit house on a friend's property to acquire spiritual power for his/her own health, prosperity, or security.

I have listed a number of common human needs that cause people to seek spiritual power, insight, and direction, to mend their erring ways, to repair relationships with people and spirits, and to seek protection and blessing. This list is not exhaustive but is the result of my research. Later I will further show how the Thai, Navajo, and Kamwe worldview assumptions shape these needs and provide solutions to them.

When these basic spiritual needs are not being met in the Christian experience, Christians are motivated to meet them in some other way. They often go to church on Sunday but to the diviner, medicine man, or spirit doctor when a spiritual need arises that the church does nothing about. Neither the traditional church nor scientific medicine has been able to do much with spirit-induced problems such as I have discussed here.

I am convinced that I serve a powerful God. We learn that God is omnipotent, but why don't we see God's power more in real life? Why hasn't the church dealt with spirit-induced sicknesses? Why haven't the spiritual-power needs been dealt with within the church framework? In the next chapter I will discuss the worldview problem that often cripples cross-cultural Christian work.

Chapter 3

Spiritual Power and Worldview

In order to understand the way in which the same felt need is met in different societies in different ways, we must examine worldview, the cultural lens through which human experience is viewed. Every society in every culture has its own worldview, the central governing set of values and basic assumptions.

DEFINING WORLDVIEW

Through the years many anthropologists have described and given valuable insights on worldview. Lorimer Fison, one of the first missionary anthropologists, realized how essential it was to see things as native peoples do, because "our mind-world is very different from theirs" (1892:149–50).

Edward Sapir, a great linguist and ethnologist, realized that behavior has an unconscious patterning:

> If we can show that normal human beings both in confessedly social behavior and often in supposedly individual behavior are reacting in accordance with deep-seated cultural patterns, and if, further, we can show that these patterns are not so much known as felt, not so much capable of conscious description as of naive practice, then we have the right to speak of the "unconscious patterning of behavior in society." (in Mandelbaum 1958:548)

Sapir was aware of what we now label worldview. People unconsciously learn the assumptions and values of the society in which they live. Language differences between societies, which were Sapir's focus, are only a part of the many variances among them. He noted that "the worlds in which different societies live are often distinct worlds, not merely the same world with different labels attached" (1929:209).

20

Robert Redfield uses the term "worldview" to refer to "the way a people characteristically look outward on the universe" (1953:85). In his study of folk society he noted that patterns of thought, attitudes toward life, conceptions of time, a mental picture of what ought to be, a people's understanding of their relationship to unseen things and to the order of things, and their view of self and others — all are included in a people's worldview.

Paul G. Hiebert's model of worldview (1985:46) presents the basic assumptions about reality in three groups that relate to the three basic dimensions of culture: the cognitive, affective, and evaluative. The cognitive assumptions define what things are "real," provide concepts of time, space, and other worlds, shape the mental categories for thinking, and give order and meaning to reality. The affective assumptions include notions of beauty, style, aesthetics, and the way people feel toward one another and life in general. The evaluative assumptions provide the standards for making judgments and also determine the priorities and allegiances of the people. The explicit belief and value systems then are built on these basic assumptions and affect all the social institutions. This model is important to the topic of this book because it underscores the emotional response to people, things, events, and the unseen.

Charles Kraft defines worldview as "the culturally structured assumptions, values and commitments underlying a people's perception of reality" (1989:20). He distinguishes between surface-level behavior and deep-level worldview:

> So as we attempt to compare cultures we need to compare them at two levels. The early anthropologists and most contemporary travelers tend to compare largely at the surface level.... If, however, we are to really understand the significance of those surface-level differences, we need to understand the deep-level assumptions and values on the basis of which people generate that surface-level behavior. (1989:182)

In order to understand behavior and different responses to felt needs, it is necessary to more thoroughly understand the deep-level assumptions.

Thus, the term "worldview," as I am using it, refers to the basic assumptions, values, and allegiances of a group of people. These assumptions affect how people perceive the self, the in-group to which they belong, outsiders, nature around them, and the nonhuman world. Worldview, formed unconsciously when people learn their own culture, makes it possible for them to feel comfortable in their environment. But it also causes discomfort and adjustment when they have to live in a different culture. A recent trip overseas (the cold showers, lack of variety in meals, a single napkin to be shared by a table full of people, main highways full of potholes, nothing starting "on time") caused me to reflect on worldview differences. I was again re-minded of the assumptions we carry with us, the emotional response to what is different based on our own assumptions, and the judgmental evaluation that automatically flows from our own assumptions. Worldview is a picture of what is and ought to be, and it provides the motivation for behavior and gives meaning to the environment.

UNDERSTANDING WORLDVIEW

Worldview provides the time and space framework, the reasons behind why things happen as they do, the options for interpreting any given activity, and the framework for evaluating all that is observed and experienced in life. Worldviews involve priorities and concepts of where loyalties are placed and what is worth risking and maybe even dying for.

Worldviews tend to conserve old ways and are resistant to change. How-ever, worldviews do change, usually quite slowly, with time and experience. Many influences bring about change in worldview, for example, forced behavioral change from the outside, exposure to new information, and ex-periences that move one to reevaluate previous concepts and values. For instance, in a society where the family is all-important, the children work with the parents so that all may benefit. When a member of the family accomplishes something, the whole family takes credit.

When a Korean family migrates to the United States, the family works together to make it. Each member of the family is needed. I have observed that Korean college students sometimes need to slow down their education in order to help in the family business. Education is an important value, how-ever, and parents are willing to sacrifice and adjust their lives for the sake of the children's education. They know that it will be to their advantage later in life if the children are educated so they can have good jobs. There is also much tension between generations when the children, influenced by Ameri-can values, expect more freedom in whom they date and marry, in how much time they spend at home, and in following the parents' wishes. The world-view of the children has undergone change due to the school system, media, and peer influence.

Each person's worldview is a bit different due to the variety of expe-riences and the processing of those experiences. As I have already noted, worldview is learned from those around us early in life. Then as a child gets older and experiences church, school, living in different environments (for example, neighborhoods or parts of the country), and organizational involve-ment (for example, sports, Scouts, band), his/her worldview may vary from the parents' worldview in some areas. Living in another country even a short time may cause one to reevaluate previous assumptions and values and consciously make changes in one's own worldview. This is a large part of why those with cross-cultural experience have a hard time fitting in when they return home. My missionary experience has left me with an appreciation of water, food, paper, and many other things. I have a hard time with those who are wasteful and also with being wasteful myself. I sometimes even find myself tearing a piece of paper in two and saving one-half of it if only half has been written on. So basic assumptions, values, and commitments do change over time and due to various circumstances.

Differences in worldview present great difficulty in communication. Customs and behavior differences are more obvious and can be dealt with, but worldview is usually unexamined and therefore largely implicit. In cross-cultural work there is often a tendency to view behavior without understanding the worldview that is related to human needs behind the action. On a recent trip to Nigeria it was called to my attention by Nigerian Christians that a Christian marriage ending in divorce was a much more serious matter than a Christian man taking a second wife. They said of the polygamist, "He did not abandon his family." Social pressure drove the divorced man out of the church, but the man with a second wife was understood.

Worldview and human felt needs are interrelated. Worldview shapes a people's felt needs; felt needs shape the worldview. To illustrate, in the white, middle-class, American worldview, individualism is an important theme. Because of this value people have a strong felt need for private space, private belongings, private time, and personal achievement. In a group-oriented society the corresponding felt need would be to blend in with the group, achieve self-identity in the group, and place the group's benefit far above self-interests.

Another example is that human felt needs for safety influence a people to form basic assumptions and values that will result in action that meets that felt need. In Western societies safety was at one time conceived of as in the hands of spiritual powers. Belief in God's protection and belief in the power of prayer were important assumptions. As worldview changed over a period of many years, with science replacing belief in spiritual powers, the basic need for security persisted, resulting in law enforcement agencies, insurance policies, and locks on houses, businesses, and cars. The assumption now is that safety is provided by using material means and is under human control.

SPIRITUAL POWER

The part of worldview focused on in this book is those beliefs, evaluations, and priorities that relate to spiritual power. The term "spiritual power" as I am using it may be either personal or impersonal. At times, spiritual power is perceived in specific material things that are often associated with religious ritual, such as a turquoise stone or guinea corn. Or it may be associated with things that represent a specific historical fact or being that has confirmed the existence of beyond-human power, for example, the Buddha image. It may be associated with spiritual beings as defined by the worldview of a society, for example, angels, evil spirits, and goddesses. Or it may be seen in a particular activity, for example, lightning or an accident. In contrast to Western secular thinking, in many parts of the world spiritual power is a part of political power, economic power, success, social power, and health.

My focus on worldview issues led me to deal with certain surface phenomena as well as deep-level phenomena. My research with the Navajo, Thai, and Kamwe included defining the spirit realm, investigating the influence of spiritual powers on daily living, locating the fears and means of protection related to spiritual power, identifying the practitioners of spiritual power, and discovering the paraphernalia that contain or represent spiritual power. My intent was to discover the basic assumptions, values, and commitments in each society. I found that one's emotional response to the environment often included seeing spiritual power in certain material goods. To illustrate, guinea corn is the staple in the Kamwe diet. On one occasion a Nigerian traveled several days with me and my family, eating all his meals with us. But when he returned home he told his friends he had not eaten since he left the village. The problem was he had not had any guinea corn. Later on, worldview investigation revealed that guinea corn is a gift of God to make people strong:

> The guinea corn myth indicates its divine origin. It serves as the fruit of the earth by which the Kamwe draw on supernatural power in rites of passage and all kinds of ritual bearing on the maintenance and restoration of peace, unity, reconciliation and the over-all harmony and cohesion of the social unit.... As God gave guinea corn and man cultivates it, what better cooperative component could there be for indicating the oneness of the supernatural and the human? (M. Kraft 1978:40)

I could no longer see guinea corn as simply something to eat. It was far more powerful than that in the eyes of the Kamwe.

Some anthropologists have focused on dynamism, the interaction of spiritual powers with human beings in daily life (Junod 1962; Van Gennep 1960; Marett 1929; Smith 1923). R. H. Codrington in 1891 wrote of the Melanesian mind as being entirely possessed by belief in a spiritual power called *mana*. He described *mana* as impersonal spiritual power in both objects and beings. However, this power is also connected with the person who directs it. A person's power and success, whether political or social, is his/her *mana:*

> This Mana is not fixed in anything, and can be conveyed in almost anything; but spirits, whether disembodied souls or supernatural beings, have it and can impart it; and it essentially belongs to personal beings to originate it, though it may act through the medium of water, or a stone, or a bone. (1891:119)

Humans do not have this power on their own; they are not *mana* themselves. But it may be said that they have *mana;* it is with them. When Melanesians are in danger, difficulty, and distress, they will naturally call on the beings in whose power they believe.

Geoffrey Parrinder, a missionary anthropologist who researched religion in Africa, noted that the concept of spiritual power is central:

> It is the importance of power, its increase or diminution, which is a constant concern in prayers and invocations, in spells and magics. All beings have their own power, and the most fortunate are those who have the greatest amount, whereas misfortune, disease and witchcraft are held to diminish power. (1969:26)

The world is seen as dynamic with one power pitted against another in daily living. African thought recognizes many different powers: divine, human, animal and plant, good and evil. Humankind is in a vital relationship with them all in a dynamic way. Parrinder found that there is no sharp dividing line between sacred and secular because the material and spiritual are intertwined.

In societies in which spiritual powers and the dynamic interaction of those powers are central to the worldview, basic spiritual-power needs must be dealt with when one becomes a Christian. The previous practices are often retained in order to meet the needs related to spiritual power. For example, when one accepts Christ but fails to deal overtly with evil spirits in a society that is keenly aware of spiritual powers, the likely result would be for one to follow previous beliefs and practices in meeting the need for protection.

FELT NEEDS, WORLDVIEW, AND REALITY

Worldview, which is owned by the group, shapes the way a human being perceives reality. The data of human experience may be seen as divisible into three parts: spiritual, human, and material. For the Thai, Navajo, and

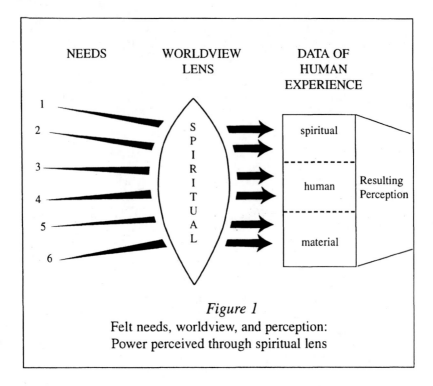

Figure 1
Felt needs, worldview, and perception:
Power perceived through spiritual lens

the Kamwe, the spiritual perspective provides the lens through which human experience is viewed (fig. 1). Figure 1 shows how human needs for power are shaped by the worldview lens. The natural and habitual way to perceive reality is through the spiritual lens.

In contrast, secular American worldview has the material as the lens to look through to view human experience (fig. 2). The material perspective, often expressed as the scientific perspective, is the way power needs are met and the way all areas of experience are dealt with. Because of this American worldview conditioning, the American Christian experiences tension between the scientific and the spiritual.

To better understand the different lenses, let us look at the need for fertile fields, a perpetuity need. According to those with the worldview in figure 1, it is a spiritual matter, so ritual interacting with spiritual powers would be performed to ensure a good crop. However, for those with the worldview illustrated in figure 2, the same need is dealt with through science. The use of fertilizer and irrigation would be seen to bring good crops, and the spiritual would be ignored. In the Navajo, Thai, and Kamwe worldviews, people see the spiritual as a great part of illness and thus require spiritual interaction for restoring health. In the American worldview people see and deal

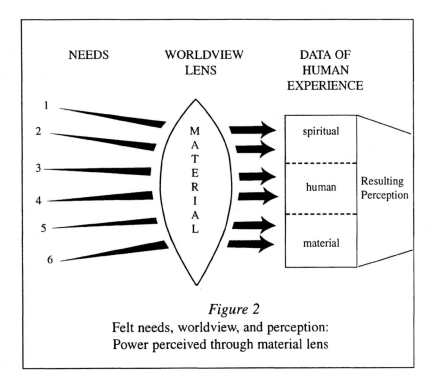

Figure 2
Felt needs, worldview, and perception:
Power perceived through material lens

with illness using science for diagnosis and treatment, usually ignoring the spiritual.

Even though the worldview lens and resulting perception provide the natural way, the habitual way, to respond to reality, there is room for change and variation. American Christians can change without totally turning their backs on science and materialism; rather, as their assumptions, values, and allegiances gradually change, so can their perspective. I have diagrammed this as a situation in which a part of the lens, as a bifocal, brings the spiritual more clearly into focus (fig. 3). The spiritual does not totally replace the material lens, but rather influences the focus in some areas. Some power needs may be perceived and dealt with through the spiritual lens and others through the material lens. This often results in conflict and tension between the material (or scientific) and the spiritual.

As modernization takes place for those looking through a spiritual lens, the material begins to influence the focus in some areas. Often change, such as the acceptance of Western medicine for certain illnesses or the use of fertilizers for getting a good crop, slowly alters the lens (fig. 4). Again, the involvement of the spiritual is lessened but not totally replaced by looking through the material lens in some areas of human experience.

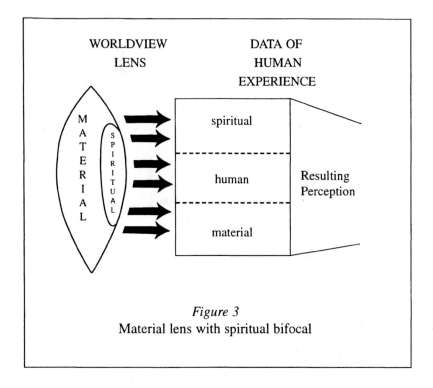

Figure 3
Material lens with spiritual bifocal

SPIRITUAL-POWER–ORIENTED SOCIETIES

In order to get a clearer picture of the worldview of spiritual-power–oriented societies, I will list some basic assumptions they characteristically hold:

1. Spiritual power, both good and evil, exists apart from human power. There are evil powers, and there are good powers.

2. Spiritual powers are active and involved in human daily experiences.

3. Human beings have limited power and hence have need for spiritual power in many areas of life.

4. Humans need good spiritual power to counteract the evil spiritual power affecting them in life.

5. There are ways for humans to access spiritual power.

6. Evil spiritual power may be used by humans to harm other humans.

7. Some spiritual powers are stronger than others.

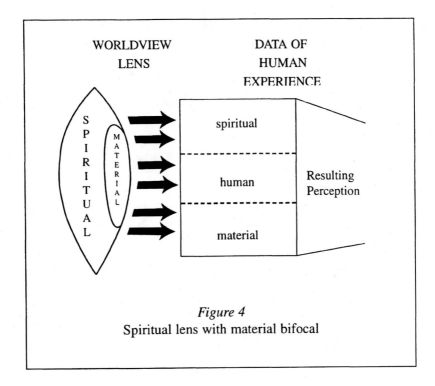

Figure 4
Spiritual lens with material bifocal

8. The strongest spiritual power wins in encounters involving more than one spiritual power.

9. Good spiritual power is to be drawn in, and evil spiritual power must be dispersed or driven away.

10. The struggle with spiritual powers continues throughout life.

For much of the world today life is full of power encounters, the confrontation between two or more spiritual powers. Spiritual powers that are involved when there is a power encounter may be personal or impersonal, evil or good, greater or lesser, within a person (spirit possession) or outside the person, autonomous or in combination, stable or transmissible. When people destroy their fetishes, they are recognizing that they have available to them a power stronger than that in the fetish. When lightning, which is perceived as a malevolent spiritual power, strikes a house and the people refuse to abandon it, but pray to God for protection, this is a power encounter. Whether or not a particular event is perceived as a confrontation of two spiritual powers is, however, in the mind of the beholder and is dependent on his/her worldview.

Alan R. Tippett in his book on Solomon Islands Christianity reports:

> When Christianity arrived the religious encounter was not between a
> pagan deity and the Christian God.... The encounter had to take place
> on the level of daily life against those powers which dealt with the rele-
> vant problems of gardening, fishing, war, security, food supply and the
> personal life crises.... In the eyes of any potential Melanesian convert
> to Christianity, therefore, the issue was one of *power in daily life*. The
> convert could not stand with the missionary and conceptualize in terms
> of psychology and Western thought-forms. Rather the missionary had
> to stand with the convert and help him to understand what Christ meant
> in terms of power encounter. (1967:5)

Christian workers must be aware of what spiritual powers are active in daily
life and on what occasions they are called on for assistance. This, then, will
enable Christ and the church to be relevant to life.

A Western worldview, with its science, knowledge, and material orientation, causes blindness to the need for recognizing spiritual powers and
the dynamic interaction taking place all the time for those in spiritual-
power–oriented societies. It also causes us to overlook the need for power
encounters. In the next chapter I will look at Western worldviews and the
problems that arise when working in societies oriented to spiritual power.

Chapter 4

The Problem with a Western Worldview

A Western worldview has often clouded the message of the gospel. In this chapter we will examine this worldview more closely, especially in areas where there is conflict with the supernaturalism in other societies. After a brief definition, we will see how Western Christians tend to be "enslaved" by their worldview. Then specific problems that arise in cross-cultural work will be discussed.

Over many years the Western world has moved from acknowledging the part that spiritual power plays in everyday living to either denying that spiritual powers exist or denying that they have any daily influence on human beings. In Western worldviews today, answers to many human needs are no longer sought from spiritual powers but are seen as attainable through human ability and science. God's power is not perceived as essential for many areas of life, and attention given to the human world far surpasses that given to the spirit world (Hiebert 1982; C. Kraft 1989:198–200). Faith in human knowledge, looking to science to resolve key problems, and specialization have pushed faith in God and his day-by-day involvement to the fringe.

WHAT IS A WESTERN WORLDVIEW?

The Enlightenment emphasized that humans are rational beings who can control their own physical and social environment. As scientific knowledge expanded, belief in the spiritual, the unseen, gradually became less important and tended to fade away. Human logic and reason became the basis for knowledge. Rationalism, the approach for understanding the natural, material world, took over and affected all areas of life. Science was seen as able to unlock the bounties of nature. More and more power was perceived to be in the hands of human beings, and only the mystical was left to religion.

31

In Western worldviews the universe is perceived as mechanistic, and human beings are perceived as masters of the universe. Nature is something to be conquered, something to overcome, improve, tear down, and rebuild in a better way. Human beings, perceiving themselves as being in charge, are primarily responsible for engineering the future. Great amounts of money, education, and energy are invested in greater control of the environment. Human attempts to control life are reflected in the availability of insurances of all kinds, preventive medicines, investment opportunities, and long-term planning. Because of this it is difficult to see and experience much of God's power in routine living. Therefore, Christianity as practiced tends to have God relegated to a comfortable, out-of-the-way place, and his power is sought only for emergency situations.

Individualism developed on the American scene early. Individuals could isolate themselves into the circle of family and friends and form that society according to their own taste. In the later part of the eighteenth century, the emphasis in child training began to shift from peace and order within the family to developing the child to be independent and self-sufficient.

> For highly individuated Americans, there is something anomalous about the relation between parents and children, for the biologically normal dependence of children on adults is perceived as morally abnormal. We have already seen how children must leave home, find their own way religiously and ideologically, support themselves, and find their own peer group. (Bellah et al. 1986:82)

To become one's own person it is seen as necessary to break free from the family, community, and inherited ways and ideas. Each person then has the freedom and responsibility to choose his/her own line of work, friends, family members to associate with, religious involvement, goals, commitments, standard of living, and level of education. People are not automatically involved in any social relationships; rather, they voluntarily choose.

In the United States between the Civil War and World War I there was rapid westward expansion and great industrial growth. New technologies in transport, manufacturing, and communications made possible the new economically integrated national society. Society was affected by the needs of the bureaucratic industrial corporations:

> The most distinctive aspect of twentieth-century American society is the division of life into a number of separate functional sectors: home and workplace, work and leisure, white collar and blue collar, public and private.... Particularly powerful in molding our contemporary sense of things has been the division between the various "tracks"

to achievement laid out in schools, corporation, government, and the professions, on the one hand, and the balancing life-sectors of home, personal ties, and "leisure," on the other.... Domesticity, love, and intimacy increasingly became "havens" against the competitive culture of work. (Bellah et al. 1986:43)

This division created a segment of life that could be labeled "religion." It related to the times in life in which one observed religious rituals and reached out for or acknowledged the existence of the spiritual world. Thus, religion has become private according to the design of the individual.

This Western worldview is clearly reflected in the Western Church. This is evident in the great emphasis on doctrine and a pervasively rationalistic approach to Christianity. Individualism often prohibits long-range commitment to the body of Christ. Because life is perceived as being in human control, God's place is usually on the fringe. Ministry to the whole person is often lost as the religious is relegated to just a corner of life. There is very little consciousness of the reality of a world of spirits and the spiritual warfare taking place today.

As people have become disillusioned with rationalism and science, interest in the spiritual has been renewed. Within Christianity a new emphasis on the spirit world is seen in the emergence of Pentecostalism, the charismatic movements in mainline churches, and more recently the development of the so-called Third Wave of the Holy Spirit. Outside Christianity, people have flowed into New Age religions and Eastern mysticism.

DOES WORLDVIEW ENSLAVE?

Since worldview is learned unconsciously and primarily belongs to the group, it does create unconscious blinders on the way a person operates. Vincent Donovan, who worked with the Masai of East Africa, a community-oriented people, writes of the exporting of individualism along with Christianity (1982:89). He notes that Christianity has consistently been interpreted from the individual viewpoint: individual responsibility, individual morality, individual vocation to leadership, self-fulfillment, individual conversion and holiness. Based on his experience, he says that the "idols of the tribe" one comes from must be cast off in order for the missionary to be effective.

Since worldview does permeate all of our customs and behavior and since we are not normally aware of our own basic assumptions, values, and allegiances, the natural/habitual way to proceed in cross-cultural situations is to follow our cultural ways. However, it is possible to consciously look for other ways of doing things based on different basic assumptions. Worldview, therefore, does not definitively determine our behavior. If we choose to come in contact with, understand, and become comfortable with other worldviews, we can consciously go against our own worldview and eventually expand/ change that worldview. For example, in some parts of the world it is possible for a whole village to own and share one car or tractor. If the village is a single clan and committed to one another, if the assumption is group ownership and cooperation for the benefit of all so that the group moves ahead together, then a single car for the village is feasible. This view is obviously very different from that held by most people in the United States — where it is often difficult for one family to share one car. However, by recognizing the assumptions and values in such a group-oriented society, the cross-cultural worker can consciously choose to work within the existing system and not promote individual ownership and competition.

A careful look at biblical truths also causes worldview dissonance for Western Christians. They have difficulty accepting at the worldview level that God is in charge, that others are as important as themselves, that an emotional response to God is as important as a rational response, and that faith in God affects all areas of life. Again, it is not impossible, but it is difficult to go against societal conditioning of values and assumptions.

Increasing rationalization and belief in science do not necessarily have to move people away from the religious and into the secular. However, it does require conscious effort to resist one's cultural programming and agree to biblical truths. Recognition of God as Creator and Controller of the universe working in and through human discoveries, inventions, and abilities allows for a compatible relationship between progress through science and faith in God.

DIFFICULTIES WITH WORKING THROUGH
A WESTERN WORLDVIEW

The issue of the need for spiritual power in daily life is a part of the philosophy of much of the world today. In areas where the great religions of the world are practiced there is usually a folk level of a given religion that is dominated by concepts of spirit power. John Newport notes that "most people in the non-Western world convert to another faith because of seeking more power" (1976:100).

Faith in God as practiced in a science- or knowledge-oriented society often fails to meet the practical needs in a spiritual-power–oriented society. Although the need for a personal relationship with Christ may not be a conscious felt need, that relationship is able to meet the felt need for spiritual power today as in Jesus' day. A relationship with Christ will in time reshape the felt needs also.

A great cultural gap exists between Westerners, who perceive the universe and social order in mechanical terms, and people in other societies who see the world as alive and relational. Paul Hiebert presents two basic analogies for analyzing religious systems: (1) to see things as living beings in relationship to one another, and (2) to see things as inanimate objects that act upon one another like parts in a machine (1982:39–43). The first, "organic" analogy sees the world in terms of living beings interacting with one another. The second, "mechanical" analogy sees things as inanimate parts of greater mechanical systems controlled by impersonal forces. Common conflicts in understanding resulting from this difference in perception include: how to treat illness, how to get the land to produce, how to be safe and secure, how to relate to each other.

Western worldview has often prevented Christianity from permeating all parts of life. Very often Westerners have failed to recognize the presence and activity of both evil and good spirits in daily life. A contemporary Igbo Christian leader writes how the God of the gospel is out of touch with many spiritual problems, and he uses the Igbo society of Nigeria as a case study:

> The Igbo, like all Africans, are very slow to disclose their religious secrets. They quietly embraced the white man's God, recognizing him as the same person who is *Chukwu* in their traditional religion. However, they tried to see him through the white man's lenses and only on Sundays, retaining allegiance to, or, on the lowest level, fear, for the traditional deities through whom they have communicated with *Chukwu* in their daily living.
>
> ...He laughs at the white man when he denies the reality of spirits and demons. He feels that the white man's God is not powerful enough to deal with these issues despite the fact that he tries to see him as the same as his *Chukwu*. He therefore resorts to his deities and ancestors through whom he contacts *Chukwu* in dealing with spirits and demons that are part of his daily experiences. (DomNwachukwu 1990:71–72)

The abstract nature of Christianity in Africa has made it come across as powerless for meeting daily needs. Due to Western worldview conditioning, cross-cultural Christian workers need to be given special training and assistance in dealing with demonic forces that work in opposition to God.

African theologian John S. Mbiti writes of the way in which traditional theology is "largely ignorant of, and often embarrassingly impotent in the face of, human questions in the churches of Africa, Latin America, parts of Asia, and the South Pacific" (1976:8). He points out that theologians are incapacitated by European education from dealing with spiritual powers. He pleads for the church to begin dealing with the daily issues people face in many parts of the world: health, healing, spirit possession, visions and dreams, witchcraft, sorcery, ancestor spirits. His own calling to ministry came originally in the form of a vision that was not taken seriously by the American missionaries.

Western worldview often causes a failure to recognize the need human beings have for power beyond themselves. The assumption that human beings are in control of their lives and environment hinders the understanding of the dependence of much of the world on spiritual power for decision making, analysis of problem areas, protection, wealth, and health. On a recent trip to the Third World I was told that angels are slow to respond to daily needs, so Christians go to the local practitioners for spiritual help. Christianity as planted in spiritual-power–oriented societies has failed to recognize the urgency for beyond-human power.

Western worldviews also limit people's ability to recognize the possibility of humans using evil spiritual power to harm other people. As a result the church is apt to do nothing about witchcraft and sorcery. Members may not even be getting the teaching that the power within them (the Holy Spirit) is greater than all other spiritual powers. Accident and illness, therefore, are treated with secular medicine and not with a spiritual-power confrontation.

Western worldviews tend to overlook or only superficially understand the passages in Scripture that speak of spiritual warfare. There is little awareness of the constant struggle of spiritual powers and no prescribed ways to counteract evil powers. This then encourages Christians to go to traditional spiritual-power sources to meet spiritual attacks.

Unconsciously looking through Western worldview lenses results in churches that lack relevance to everyday living in places where much spiritual activity is perceived. The forms, the rituals, the teachings, and the practices give the impression of serving a powerless God.

PART II

THE PERSPECTIVE

Chapter 5

Theology and the Powers

Currently we are being forced to face both in missions and on the home front the reality of the spirit world and the supernatural. This is seen in the Western world in the popularity of seeking spiritual power through Eastern religions, the New Age movement, and "out-of-body" experiences. In the Two-Thirds World the consciousness of the spirit world and its power continues to be very real even after people have become Christians. This present consciousness is reminiscent of New Testament understandings.

This chapter deals with how we make sense of the principalities and powers of the Bible. Can these be dismissed as first-century, prescientific superstition? In this chapter, I deal with the Christian definition of Satan and evil powers, including the views of some theologians who have researched and written on the powers. This is followed by a brief discussion of the spiritual powers in Christian tradition. I then present my own theological position.

In many societies the great god has two faces, good and evil. Or individual deities have opposite poles in a single being: benevolence and malevolence, creativity and destructiveness. Or the independent existence of evil spirits accounts for much of the evil in the world. Around the world blackness and darkness are almost always associated with evil: with death, blindness, the underworld, nocturnal activities of spirit beings and robbers, despair, sin, poison, the plague. These worldwide similarities dealing with evil as experienced in daily living suggest a common human struggle in dealing with the tension between good and evil within the individual and within society.

CHRISTIAN DEFINITION OF THE POWERS

Jeffrey Burton Russell, a medievalist who has for twenty years studied the problem of evil, has researched the historical development of the concepts of evil and its personification and has authored a critically acclaimed series on the history of the devil (1977, 1981, 1984, 1986, 1988). He asserts the reality of the devil and sees him as behind the evil in the world. Russell defines evil as follows:

> Evil is meaningless, senseless destruction. Evil destroys and does not build; it rips and it does not mend; it cuts and it does not bind. It strives always and everywhere to annihilate, to turn to nothing. (1977:23)

He defines the devil, then, "as a personality with consciousness, will, and intelligence, whose intent is entirely focused upon causing suffering and misery" (1981:274). Though there is no idea of a single personification of evil in most religions (for example, Hinduism, Buddhism, and ancient Greco-Roman religions), four major religions have had a real devil: Mazdaism (Zoroastrianism), ancient Hebrew religion (but not modern Judaism), Christianity, and Islam (Russell 1988:4).

From earliest times the Hebrews recognized the presence of Satan and evil spirits. But scholars have pointed to Zoroastrian influence after the Babylonian exile as the factor that sharpened the concept of spirits, angels, and Satan in Judaism. William LaSor notes that the discovery of the Dead Sea Scrolls has shown Zoroastrian influence in the Qumran literature:

> Some of the most striking parallels to Jewish-Christian eschatology can be shown to be very late developments in Zoroastrianism. On the other hand it would not do violence to a high view of inspiration to admit that God could have used Zoroastrianism as a means of stimulating the Jewish mind to think on these subjects even as he used Hellenism to prepare the Jewish mind for the Christian revelation (witness Saul of Tarsus). (1984:1202)

In the Qumran documents and in Zoroastrianism, the devil is the head of a host of evil spirits who, like the good spirits, are arranged in orders and ranks. The role of both the Hebrew devil and the Persian devil is to seduce, accuse, and destroy. Though for both the Hebrews and the Persians the cosmos is divided into two forces, light and darkness, in the Hebrew system the two are not of equal power.

Satan occupies a central position in the New Testament as the chief enemy of Christ. His importance is shown by the variety of titles given him. In the New Testament these include "the enemy," "Beelzebub," "the god of this world," "the tempter," "the accuser," "the evil one," "the ruler of this world," and "the prince of demons." He is to be regarded as a powerful spiritual being. Christians are members of the kingdom of God but must continue to live on earth and be at war with the kingdom of Satan.

The first-century world agreed on the reality of evil spirits and Satan. In the Gospels it is Luke who portrays the message of Christian authority over the power of Satan most vividly: Jesus' testing in the wilderness by Satan, Jesus' releasing some of the oppressed from captivity, Christians' success in casting out demons and healing, and the success of Christ in the conversion of Saul. Susan Garrett exegetes the role of Satan in the cosmic and earthly drama involving Jesus:

> Luke has taken pains to show that behind the defeated enemies stood none other than the Devil. Thus these incidents, like the ones involving magicians, point beyond the visible human arena to the invisible spiritual one, where the Holy Spirit repeatedly meets the spirit of the Devil and causes it to shrink or to flee. (1989:103)

A real spiritual battle is being waged between the powers of Christ and the powers of Satan.

Paul writes of spiritual realities with which he and his fellow Christians have personal acquaintance. The idea of spiritual powers and their subjugation to Christ is built into "the very fabric of Paul's thought, and mention of them is found in every epistle except Philemon" (Caird 1956:viii). Clinton E. Arnold in his study of spiritual powers presents Paul as a man of his times affirming the existence of the spirit world.

> Paul never showed any sign of doubt regarding the real existence of the principalities and powers. He saw them as angelic beings belonging to Satan's kingdom. Their aim is to lead humanity away from God through direct influence on individuals as well as through wielding control over the world religions and various other structures of our existence. (1992:169)

The spirit world was recognized as exercising influence over virtually every aspect of life. The practice of magic was common for obtaining access to and use of spiritual power, a power gained by manipulating the spirit world. Furthermore, the magician was often seen as the "minister of Satan."

Hendrikus Berkhof has noted that two things are always true of the powers: (1) they are personal, spiritual beings; and (2) they influence events on earth, especially events within nature (1962:11). He sees Paul as concerned about the powers in their role in the human drama, focusing on the structures of earthly existence. Heinrich Schlier describes these principalities and powers as follows:

They do not merely possess power and the other attributes, they are power. They are not just something or somebody, and also have power. They exist as power, etc. That is what they are called, and they get these names because that is how they manifest themselves and their being. (1961:19)

When these spirits penetrate the world to exercise their power, they are actively working in people and institutions.

Walter Wink carries this institutional involvement of the powers to an extreme. His interest is in the evils that afflict society and the church. Wink views these powers not as spiritual but as "the inner aspect of material or tangible manifestations of power" (1984:104). He sees no separation between heavenly and earthly entities:

"Spiritual" here means the inner dimension of the material, the "within" of things, the subjectivity of objective entities in the world. Instead of the old dualism of matter and spirit, we can now regard matter and spirit as united in one indivisible reality, distinguishable in two discrete but interrelated manifestations. (1984:107)

According to Wink none of the "spiritual realities" has an existence independent of its material counterpart.

The thesis underlying his handling of the data is that unless the context further specifies, the terms for power are taken in their most comprehensive sense, meaning both divine and human, both heavenly and earthly, both good and evil. Wink presents Paul as having demythologized the powers so that the spiritual essences were no longer in his mind:

The New Testament is not fond of the spiritualistic reductionism of later Christendom, which limited the Powers to hostile spirits in the air. The New Testament prefers to speak of the powers only in their concretions, their structural inertia, their physical embodiments in history. The Powers that Paul was most concerned with did not fly; they were carved in stone. (1984:82)

However, New Testament writers use the word "authority" (*exousia*) to refer to a human power on one occasion and to spiritual power on another. This fact, in my estimation, counters Wink's concept that the word refers to both simultaneously. The context determines which meaning from the range of meanings is appropriate. In my opinion Wink is imposing a post-Enlightenment mind-set on first-century writing.

Wink reflects the controlling influence of his scientific worldview as he thinks about the biblical references on the powers. He betrays this when he asserts, "It is as impossible for most of us to believe in the real existence of demonic or angelic powers as it is to believe in dragons, or elves, or a flat world" (1984:4). He notes that whatever we cannot fit into our material categories we label as "superstition." Though Wink recognizes radical evil in the world, he cannot conceive of evil spirits or Satan apart from the structures and the people who operate them. The influence of Western secular assumptions is evident in the way he approaches biblical interpretation.

Wink (1986) analyzes Satan as the "collective symbolization of evil," the "collective weight of human fallenness." According to him it is human beings who have made Satan "the god of this world" (2 Cor. 4:4) by their practice of constantly giving over the world to him as a consequence of willfully seeking their own good without reference to any higher good. He sees Satan as the symbol of the spirit of an entire society alienated from God. Laboring his point since it is far from obvious, he says:

> When in Luke 4:6 Satan declares that he can give Jesus all the kingdoms of the world and their glory, he is not lying; "for it has been delivered to me, and I give it to whom I will." God *permits* Satan such power, but has not handed it over to him; *we have delivered it,* as a consequence of all the consciously or unconsciously evil choices we have individually and collectively made against the long-range good of the whole. (1986:24)

Satan in Wink's eyes is an archetypal image of the universal experience of evil — his fall has taken place in the human psyche. Though Wink recognizes the reality of human sinful nature and alienation from God, he sees Satan, demons, and the powers as entering the world after human societies had reached a certain threshold of density, complexity, and conflict (1992:39). Wink's concern is how this archetypal reality of evil is currently manifesting itself in persons and in society. He presents the church's peculiar calling as discerning and engaging "both the structure and the spirituality of oppressive institutions" (1992:84).

A comment by Jeffrey Russell is relevant to Wink's extensive attempts to explain in modern terms the obvious intent of New Testament authors. Russell writes:

> Biblical criticism often intrudes contemporary assumptions into our understanding of the past. This blurs efforts to get at a literal understanding of Scripture, for the best definition of "literal" is the original intent of the author. To get at that original intent means scraping away

not only encrustations of tradition but also encrustations of current historical assumptions. (1988:260)

Arnold, having researched power and magic in Ephesians, contends that Wink failed to take into account the importance of the magical tradition in the first century:

> The presence of magic in the Hellenistic world blatantly contradicts the demythologizing trend that Wink sees in the first century. The practice of magic implies a vibrant and flourishing belief in evil spiritual forces — forces that magicians in no way identified with humans or institutions. The magician believed in personal spirits that bore names. The spirits could be called upon to appear or to perform certain tasks. The spirits were greatly feared by the common people of the Hellenistic world in the first century A.D. (1989:50)

This consciousness of spirits and magic on the part of the first readers of the New Testament assures us that it was personal (not institutional) spirit powers that were in view in such contexts as Col.1:16; Eph.1:20ff.; 6:12. Arnold points to both the magical papyri and Jewish tradition to support this contention (1989:191).

Arnold demonstrates that Eph. 2:2–3 depicts the coexistence of two categories of power constituting the present age (1989:132–33). One power is the "flesh," which leads people away from God and is opposed to the working of the Holy Spirit. The other is demonic power, which exerts power over people — "the authority of the air."

EVIL SPIRITS IN CHRISTIAN TRADITION

Historical study of Christian tradition shows that there has been a continuous belief in evil spirits and Satan. As we have seen, personal spiritual powers were a reality to the Christians of the first century. This reality was such that Justin Martyr, one of the earliest Christian theologians (born about 100), saw a cosmic struggle between Satan and his followers and God and his followers. He perceived that persecution of the Christians was through those who were in the service of Satan. Demons provoked hatred, lies, and false accusations and encouraged the pagan persecutions.

By the third century the Western Church practiced exorcism as an invariable part of the rite of baptism. Before candidates could be accepted into the body of Christ, evil spirits had to be exorcized from their souls:

Unbaptized persons needed exorcizing because Satan held lordship
over humanity from the time of Adam and Eve. Underlying exorcism
is the assumption that even after the Incarnation Satan retains certain
powers over the material world as well as over fallen humans. (Russell
1988:121)

As a part of the baptismal rite, the priest marked the sign of the cross on
the candidate's brow and also anointed him/her with holy oil to keep the
demons away.

In *The Life of St. Anthony* (written about 360), Athanasius describes
the constant struggle against Satan and his powers in the monk's training.
Athanasius tells many stories of demons taking on visible forms and attack-
ing the monks. He records that Satan tempted Anthony by suggesting all the
benevolent donations he could make if he kept his money, by instilling in
his mind images of wealth, banquets, and glory, by causing doubt about the
monastic vocation through introducing images of the dangers and discom-
forts of life in the desert, and by taking the tempting form of a sensuous
young woman. Anthony was also awakened by horrible shrieking noises and
the walls of his hut shaking, followed by demons in the forms of lions, bears,
leopards, and wolves. The higher the monks rose in their quest for God, the
more intensely Satan attacked them.

In the early Middle Ages, three things were evident in the attitudes toward
and beliefs in spiritual powers. First was the fear of evil spirits. Monks taught
the laity about demonic powers for the express purpose of frightening their
congregations into avoiding sin. Second, was the attitude of ridicule. Folklore
and legend made Satan seem ridiculous and impotent. Third, there was a
seriousness about the spirit world:

Lucifer and his followers are active always and everywhere. They
cause mental and physical illness; they steal children, shoot arrows
at people, attack them with cudgels, or leap upon their backs. They
enter the body through every orifice, especially the mouth during
yawning and the nose during sneezing. They haunt graveyards, ruins,
and houses. Ghosts appeared in medieval folklore as souls on leave
from purgatory, but Christian theology more commonly assumed that
they were actually demons taking on the shapes of the dead. (Russell
1988:115)

While theology insisted that Satan and demons could be defeated only by
calling on the name of Christ, folklore tamed the terror by allowing humans
to trick these powers with native wit and guile.

Theology began to move away from experience through scholasticism, which dominated intellectual life from 1000 to 1300. Anselm in his writing and teaching did much to reduce Satan's role in theology. He emphasized the free will in Lucifer's choice and also humankind's free will. God created human beings and angels to conform to justice and be in harmony with the cosmos and with him. God is only indirectly responsible for the freely willed choices of human beings. The tightly logical systems of the scholastics found little need for Satan. But at the same time, in European culture as a whole and in literature and legend the figure of Satan grew in strength. Dante, the greatest medieval poet, featured Satan in his *Divine Comedy* as a powerful force operating throughout both hell and earth. In his mystical poem every being in the cosmos moves either toward God or toward Satan.

The theology of Martin Luther demonstrated his deep personal concern with Satan. He saw God allowing Satan to work evil; in any evil event both Satan and God were active. There is a difference, however, in their motive: God has an ultimately benevolent purpose in every act, but Satan's aim is always to destroy. Luther's own experience reflected his worldview, which saw each individual caught in a tension between Christ and the devil. He reported that Satan attempted to prohibit him from doing God's work in many ways. He rattled around behind Luther's stove; at Wartburg castle he pelted nuts at the roof and rolled casks down the stairwell; he appeared to Luther in the form of a serpent and the form of a star; he disputed with Luther like a scholastic. Luther was even known to throw an inkwell at Satan.

In the late Middle Ages (1400–1700) both nominalism and mysticism tended to downplay Satan's power, but witchcraft was perceived to be real in Western society. Writers, judges, and theologians assumed that witches existed all over Europe, and these witches were linked in one great conspiracy under Satan's rule. Though not all of the accusations were false, things got far out of hand:

> The witch craze constitutes one of the most important episodes in the history of the Devil. Belief in his immediate and terrible powers was revived throughout society to an extent unsurpassed even at the time of the desert fathers. And it revealed the most terrible danger of belief in the Devil: the willingness to assume that those whom one distrusts or fears are the servants of Satan and fitting targets of hatred and destruction.... The witch craze at its height in the Renaissance and Reformation periods in both Catholic and Protestant regions and peaking in the period from 1550 to 1650, eventually faded owing to the philosophical ideas of the Enlightenment and the disgust that the patent excesses of the witch hunters had engendered among responsible and reflective people. (Russell 1984:301)

The terror of witchcraft brought about persecution of supposed witches, and as many as a hundred thousand victims were killed. The discrediting of witchcraft was largely responsible for the decline in the belief in Satan.

Russell presents the turning inward of the Christian conscience in the sixteenth century as a reason for the growth of Satan's power. This was found both in Protestantism and in the new introspective character of Catholicism typified by Ignatius Loyola:

> Earlier ages had seen the Devil's opponent as God, Christ, or the whole Christian community. If attacked by Satan, you could at least feel part of a great army upon whose hosts you could call for aid. But now it was you versus the Devil; you alone, the individual, who had the responsibility for fending him off. No one denied that the grace of Christ protected the faithful, but the new introspection placed upon the individual the burden of examining his soul for signs of a weak faith that would invite the Devil in. (Russell 1986:31)

This individualistic emphasis on self-reliance and competition left the Christian exposed and fearful of Satan's powers.

John Milton's *Paradise Lost,* written in the mid–seventeenth century, gave a magnificent portrait of Satan based on Scripture. This poetic account of salvation in Christ helped keep the image of Satan powerful in Western minds long after the theological belief had faded.

During the late nineteenth and early twentieth centuries, however, materialist assumptions virtually overwhelmed a serious belief in evil:

> In society as a whole, beyond theological circles, belief in the existence of both God and the Devil has drastically declined since the eighteenth century, less because of theological arguments than because of the growing predominance of materialism. Although decline of belief in radical evil has not been accompanied by any noticeable decline in the action of radical evil, by the 1980s belief in the Devil remained strong only among conservative Christians and Muslims — and a few occultists. (Russell 1988:261)

The Catholic Church continued the rite of exorcism and specified standard tests of the validity of alleged cases of demon possession. Conservative Protestants also defended the reality of Satan's personal existence. On the other hand, mainstream, liberal Protestant theology tended to deny or at least ignore Satan. This was not based on biblical scholarship as much as on embarrassment over belief in spiritual entities in the midst of an increasingly materialist society.

C. S. Lewis in his writings depicts Satan and demons seeking opportunities for evil in everyday human weaknesses in an attempt to detach Christians from God. He portrays demons, motivated by both fear and hunger, roaming the world seeking human souls to devour.

In spite of opposition from theologians, scientists, and others, the concept of Satan is very much alive today:

> Well-intended efforts to reform human nature by education or legislation have so far failed, and rather spectacularly, as they break like waves against the rock of radical evil. We have direct perception of evil, of deliberate malice and desire to hurt, constantly manifesting itself in governments, in mobs, in criminals, and in our own petty vices. Many people seem to have the additional experience that behind all this evil, and directing it, is a powerful, transhuman, or at least transconscious, personality. This is the Devil. (Russell 1981:222)

Russell concludes that the idea is more alive now than it has been for many decades because of the ineradicable nature of perversity evident in the twentieth century.

MY THEOLOGICAL FOUNDATION

My own theology starts from the fact that God created all that is, and he created it good. He made human beings in his own image. Both angels and humans were created to serve God. Both angels and humans were given their choice of doing good or evil. Human beings were made a little lower than God himself and were placed in charge of all God created on the earth (Psalm 8). Satan was a powerful angel who fell from heaven (Isa. 14:12–15) and presently is the "prince of the power of the air" (Eph. 2:1–2) and roams the earth like a lion looking for someone to devour (1 Pet. 5:8).

The fall of Adam and Eve in the Garden of Eden marked for all time humankind's disobedience to God. It allowed evil to come into all humans, which brought separation from God. Humankind since has been prone to do evil and sin. Only through the birth, death, and resurrection of God's son, Jesus, have humans been restored to their rightful position with God. However, humans must choose to follow God and be obedient to him. Satan, with his followers (other angels who have chosen evil), also is seeking human beings and trying to get them to follow him. His intent is to destroy all he can and definitely work to keep humans from following and being obedient to God. So there is a tension in all human beings between good and evil.

I do not agree with Wink's analysis of evil powers existing only in persons, institutions, structures, and systems. The radical evil we see in society around us is the result of human beings' sinful nature, their refusal to choose to follow God's way, and the activity of Satan and his followers tempting and at times effectively controlling human beings. These all three affect the institutions and structures of society that are in the control of humans. I see Satan and evil spirits existing outside of persons and structures but influencing the structures as they influence the people involved in those structures. It is possible for evil spirits to reside within humans, as seen in Matt. 10:1; 12:43–45; Acts 5:1–11; 16:16–18. Satan certainly strategizes to destroy through capitalizing on human fallenness and weakness. The result is the evil we see around us in the world. Christ, too, wants to change the world and has chosen to work through those who have committed themselves to him to combat Satan's power on earth.

Salvation through Christ has made Christians members of the kingdom of God, but living on this earth where Satan is ruler creates much difficulty. Christ's death and resurrection have brought victory and freedom to people who follow him (Heb. 2:14–16). However, the standards (norms) of this world do not line up with God's norms. It is important for Christians to be aware of the spiritual battle that has been ultimately won by Christ (Col. 2:15) and of the spiritual battle that is currently going on in this world. Christians need to actively work to take away from Satan's kingdom and expand the borders of the kingdom of God, to firmly stand against evil and obediently work with God and through his Spirit to overcome Satan and his work.

Chapter 6

Spiritual Power and the Bible

A Western worldview has conditioned us to focus on the knowledge given in the Bible and the correct understanding of the doctrines set forth therein. Since our scientific approach to life and our confidence in human beings' ability to manage life do not allow much credence to the daily effects of spiritual power, our focus in studying and teaching the Bible does not stress a God of power. There is a certain amount of awe as to how God worked in biblical times but very little understanding of how he might meet people's spiritual-power needs today. For this reason we will look at how God used his power in working with his people, who had many of the basic assumptions listed (in chap. 3) for spiritual-power–oriented societies.

Bible courses teach how God is omnipresent, omniscient, and omnipotent, but the meaning of that for everyday living often is overlooked. The same kind of teaching is a part of Bible schools and seminaries in all parts of the world — they focus on knowing the facts. However, it is very important in spiritual-power–oriented societies to deal with the greatness of God's power and how he uses it.

A recent class on power encounters for Nigerian church leaders was a great revelation to them about the nature of God. The course showed how it is God's practice to deal with the existing powers. Since he has already defeated Satan (Col. 2:15), he will be victorious. Letting God show himself through power encounters in order to strengthen believers or to show nonbelievers that he is all-powerful was a relatively new concept. As citizens of the kingdom of God living in this world — the kingdom of Satan — Christians need to be ready for battle (C. Kraft 1991b). Satan does not want to give up his territory to the power of God, so Christians with the Holy Spirit in them are a very real threat to him. The common missionary attitude of questioning the existence of evil powers has not helped the people or even the Christian leaders in spiritual-power–oriented societies claim God's authority over the evil spiritual powers around them. Hopefully this chapter will help in our understanding of God and challenge the reader to seek further enlightenment by searching the Scriptures for a God of power.

In the Old Testament, Israel is called out from the nations to be God's people, to be holy and separate for the Lord, and to be a witness to the world. This concept of peoplehood is developed throughout all of Scripture, with the people of God presented as a corporate, interacting, sharing, worshiping community in the world. In the New Testament the concept "people of God," with its promises and responsibilities, is transferred to the church. God's continuing method of communicating himself to human beings is through his people.

In order to better understand God's use of his power in a world with other existing supernatural powers, I will focus on the scriptural presentation of the people of God in their network of relationships to each other, to outsiders, to God, and to other spiritual entities. The periods as I have divided them are according to culture and worldview: (1) the patriarchal period, (2) the exodus, (3) the period of the judges, (4) the monarchy, (5) the exile, and (6) the first century c.e. The first five are treated in reference to the Old Testament and the last in reference to the New Testament. In each period I am particularly interested in the basic assumptions, values, and specific human needs. My concern is to understand more clearly how God met his people within their culture, dealt with them, and brought about a transformation in their lives. These meetings are power encounters and are common occurrences throughout Scripture.

G. Ernest Wright has suggested that the Bible should more accurately be referred to as "the Acts of God" because the primary means by which God communicates with humans is by his acts:

> The focus of attention is not upon the Word of God in and for itself so that it can be frozen, so to speak, within a system of dogmatic propositions. The Word leads us, not away from history, but to history and to responsible participation within history. The Bible thus is not primarily the Word of God, but the record of the Acts of God, together with the human response thereto. (1952:107)

Communicologists today emphasize how much of the meaning of words is carried in the accompanying actions. Thus the Bible leads us to participation and understanding of God through his actions, and then from that our theological statements are inferred. We will examine some of God's actions and how humans responded with specific worldviews and felt needs in evidence.

Because the focus of this book is on spiritual power, I intend to examine specific power encounters in Scripture. Two other types of encounters

that surround and flow from power encounters are truth and commitment encounters (C. Kraft 1991b:258–265). Both of these have traditionally been
in focus in the evangelical world. Commitment encounters are struggles,
seen throughout Scripture, over whether to follow other gods or to be
faithful to God (Josh. 24:14, 15). Truth encounters involve accepting and
knowing truth in God and his acts, for example, creation, his leading his
people to the promised land, and his incarnation in Jesus. The actual value
and truth in idols and other gods, or in evaluating humans from the outside and not the heart, provide conflict and encounter with God's truth. At
times God uses his power to gain people's allegiance and to make clear his
truth (Exod. 3:1–12; Matt. 20:29–34). Other times he shows his power as
a result of a person's allegiance or of a person's recognition of his truth
(Matt. 5:25–34; 8:1–3; Luke 7:2–10). And at times failure to accept God's
truth and/or failure to give allegiance to him prompted God to use his
power seemingly against his people, for example, in the captivity (2 Chron.
36:13–21).

OLD TESTAMENT ACTS SHOWING GOD'S POWER

My study of the role of spiritual powers in a variety of worldviews has
confirmed the tremendous importance of the Old Testament to many societies of the world today. It is regrettable that there are many languages into
which the Old Testament has not been translated, one reason for this being
the greater importance the West places on the New Testament. Many times
the Hebrew worldview is closer to that of the receptor culture. Thus an understanding of God comes more clearly through the Old Testament in the great
variety of power demonstrations that God uses to show his people that he is
a God of power.

The Patriarchal Period

In the time of Abraham the patriarchal deity was common among tribal
peoples. The patriarch would consciously choose as his personal god a deity with whom he would enter a special covenantal relationship (Wright
1960:32). The god then became an actual member of the clan and could
be called "father" or "brother." All members of the clan were accordingly
children, brethren, or kinsmen of the god. Indeed, the god was the head of
the house. Any treaties or legal agreements made between clans included
the gods, who through their involvement made the covenant absolutely
binding.

How natural then for God to reveal himself in the people's patterns of thought. God used the covenant with each of the patriarchs (Gen. 12:1–3; 17:2–8; 22:16; 26:3–5; 28:13–15; 35:9–12). He promised his blessing, the gift of land, his protection, and many descendants. He expected from them their obedience.

On occasion the Lord doubtless spoke directly to the individual, but often he spoke in visions or dreams (to Abraham, Genesis 15; to Isaac, Gen. 26:23–25; to Jacob, Gen. 28:10–15; 31:11–13; 46:2, 3). All ancient nations attached great importance to dreams. Alfred Guillaume notes that the Akkadians regarded dreams as equally authoritative as omens and believed that all dreams were sent by the gods (1938:48).

God on many occasions showed his power and presence during the patriarchal period. When Abraham and Sarah were in Egypt and the king took Sarah as his wife, God sent terrible diseases on him and on the people of his palace (Gen. 12:17–20). When Hagar was in deep distress, the angel of the Lord appeared to her (Gen. 16:7–12; 21:17–19). At one point when God wanted to talk to Abraham at Mamre, he came to him in his tent in human form (Genesis 18).

God's angel went before Abraham's servant in the search for a suitable wife for Isaac (Genesis 24). His power and provision made it possible for Sarah and Rebecca to bear children (Gen. 18:13, 14; 25:21). God's power was seen by the people when he killed Er, Judah's first son, because of his evil conduct (Gen. 38:7), and also Onan, his second son (Gen. 38:10). Joseph recognized God's power and provision for him (Gen. 40:16; 50:19, 20). These are only a few of the ways and times that God made his power felt by the patriarchs. It is clear that he was in touch with their specific needs and ready to use his power on their behalf. However, at times God did not choose to show his power as we might expect, for example, when Joseph was sold into slavery and when Jacob and his family had to move because of famine to Egypt, where they became an enslaved people. God has the full picture in view, and he alone chooses when to step in with his power.

The patriarchal period was characterized by God choosing to bless and direct one specific extended family over several generations through specific individuals. The biblical record of the vicissitudes of this clan shows clearly a powerful God who reveals himself and makes promises which he faithfully carries out. On occasion this clan's faith in him and their obedience to his will are impressive. God as seen by the patriarchs was not restricted to a fixed place of residence; he was not a local or territorial God, rather the one who accompanied his people and looked out for their welfare. He revealed himself in power to deepen their relationship, to give protection and direction, and to establish a people who would be a witness to the world.

The Exodus

In the period of the exodus, Moses accepted and believed in "the God of our fathers" and the covenant from the patriarchal period. God in his sovereign act then delivered his people from Egypt, where they had been enslaved. Through the covenant and the Decalogue and the teaching that followed, God made clear his purpose in his act of redemption. Israel became an established people, whose religion had its beginning as a national religion.

Jacob had emigrated to Egypt with his sons because of famine in Palestine. The descendants of Abraham had been scattered as slave labor throughout the land when God chose Moses as his messenger/prophet to bring his chosen people out of slavery in Egypt. God achieved this deliverance through a series of power encounters before the king of Egypt (Exod. 7:8–14:31). The king's magicians were able to do some of the same things that God gave Moses and Aaron instruction and power to perform. However, God remained in control and increasingly showed his power. The theme "Let my people go!" and the declaration that the Egyptians "shall know that I am the Lord" showed clearly his purpose (Exodus 5–11). Through these numerous power demonstrations and the faithfulness and obedience of his servant, Moses, God was bringing forth his people in history.

As the Israelites were followed by the menacing Egyptian army, the Lord's response was given by Moses: "The Lord will fight for you, and there is no need for you to do anything" (Exod. 14:14). In the crossing of the Red Sea, God shows himself as one who has power over nature and the enemy (Exod. 14:21–31). He alone was the warrior and he alone was king, as expressed so beautifully in Exodus 15, the song of victory:

> I will sing to the Lord,
>   because he has won a glorious victory;
> he has thrown the horses and their riders
>   into the sea....
> The Lord is a warrior;
>   the Lord is his name....
>
> Your right hand, Lord, is awesome in power;
>   it breaks the enemy in pieces....
>
> You blew on the sea and the water piled up high;
>   it stood up straight like a wall;
>   the deepest part of the sea became solid....

One breath from you, Lord,
    and the Egyptians were drowned;
    they sank like lead in the terrible water.

Lord, who among the gods is like you:
    Who is like you, wonderful in holiness?
    Who can work miracles and mighty acts like
        yours?...

You, Lord, will be king for ever and ever.
                    (Exod. 15:1b, 3, 6, 8, 10, 11, 18)

Then followed forty years in the desert away from outside pressures: a time of chastening the initial generation and then sharpening the relationship between God and the desert-born second generation. God often brought "signs" to show the people that Moses had divine authority for his actions (Exod. 15:25; 17:8–11). God showed his power to the leaders of Israel by having Moses strike the rock, so that drinking water could come out of it (Exod. 17:5, 6). As God showed his power through lightning and thunder, smoke and fire, the people who had been commanded to gather for worship were filled with fear (Exod. 19:9–19). Though God did not use his power to make life always easy for the Israelites as they might have wished, he was in control and faithful. Throughout Moses' experiences we see that when God talks to human beings, he speaks through them to others.

The Period of the Judges

The Israelites first entered the land of Canaan under the leadership of Joshua. They entered whenever they could peacefully, but many times they were in war. At times they completely overthrew those who lived in the land, and other times they lived side by side with those who had been there before them. The land was divided among the twelve tribes, who appeared to act independently or in small groups.

As Israel was getting settled in the land of Canaan, the Israelite judges began to appear, providing the much-needed leadership. The Ammonite, Moabite, and Edomite neighbors of Israel were ruled at this time by kings, and there was much unrest in the area. One group would overthrow another and rule them for several years; then another battle and a change of rule would take place.

God raised up judges to provide leadership for his people, and they were in direct contact with him. Sometimes the divine contact required public signs and acknowledgment prior to the act of deliverance in order to affirm the judge's authority. The judges were appointed for their task *ad hoc,* and their job was not hereditary or transferable. The relationship between the leader and the people was not based on formal rules. Rather the judges arose from time to time with God's message to proclaim. They followed one another but did not constitute an unbroken chain. This is not surprising because in order for one of these judges to appear there had to be a combination of personal qualities and the necessary historical circumstances as well.

We see in the book of Judges a constant cycle of defection from Yahweh, followed by a time of foreign oppression, from which the people of God were delivered. Norman Snaith writes of the repeated apostasy of Israel:

> The people turned aside from worshipping Jehovah and they bowed down to other gods. Then "the anger of the Lord was kindled against them," and "he delivered them into the hands of the spoilers." God sent them a deliverer, who rescued them from the spoilers, and as long as that judge lived, all was well. But when that judge died, the Israelites went astray again, and the same cycle followed. (1957:127–28)

At one point, after the people of Israel had sinned against God and worshiped other gods, God let the Midianites rule them for seven years. He then sent an angel to Gideon as he was secretly threshing wheat to inform him that he was to be God's means of rescuing Israel this time. Gideon doubted and needed proof on two occasions. God in his power showed his presence and will by sending fire that consumed the meat and bread (Judg. 6:21) and by the unusual presence or absence of dew on the wool Gideon laid out (Judg. 6:36–40). Gideon, following God's command to cut down the size of his army, was told by God that the encounter was to be between God and the enemy. The victory was God's even before it was fought (Judg. 7:19–24).

A very interesting power encounter occurred between the God of Israel and the god Dagon of the Philistines (1 Samuel 5). The Philistines, having won the battle with the Israelites and having captured the Ark of the Covenant, placed the ark next to their god Dagon in order to have double spiritual power. Uncontrollable events followed involving the falling and breaking of the statue of Dagon and the people of the area having tumors. God demonstrated to both the Philistines and the Israelites in terms they could understand that his power was greater than that of the god Dagon, and he was not to be controlled by human beings.

Many times God won battles for the Israelites as they entered and possessed the land of Canaan. The evidence of God working with nature to the benefit of Israel spoke of his greatness and power: "The earth shook" (Judg. 5:4, 5), "The stars fought" (Judg. 5:20), "The sun stood still" (Josh. 10:12ff.). The Israelites' close contact with other groups in Canaan and the resulting erosion of their faith and seduction to foreign gods led to God warring against his people and judging them. Yet he repeatedly delivered them through the judges.

The Monarchical Period

Up to the monarchical period the political organization of Israel had been strikingly different from that of the surrounding people. For almost two hundred years Israel was held together by no central political leader but by a religious covenant. However, the time came when the pressures from outside became so strong that the people felt they needed a centralized government like other nations. The Israelites insisted that they have a king to judge them and go out before them and fight their battles (1 Sam. 8:6–20).

In setting up the kingship of Israel the power base was ideally to be faith in and obedience to God (Deut. 17:18–20). The king was not to rely on military, economic, and diplomatic power like other nations. He was seen "as the representative of God upon earth, appointed by Yahweh and responsible to him" (Ringgren 1966:233). He was seen by the people as a sacred person with wisdom from God. Theoretically, however, his job was not to enact laws, for in Israel the law was prior to kingship and superior to it. Furthermore, the law was given by Yahweh to set guidelines for fulfilling the demands of the covenant, which embraced the whole people. As a result, the king could not claim credit for the law; he could only administer it.

However, with the selection of Saul as the first king, a departure from this ideal was almost immediately apparent. In Saul's disobedience to God, an "evil spirit sent by the Lord" fell on him (1 Sam. 16:14; 19:9). Because Israel and its king did not follow the Lord, the monarchical period became the most warlike period in Israel's history. More often than not God fought against his people rather than for them.

It was David who made the monarchy an influential institution. In much of his reign, God was in control and David was in subjection to him. David often inquired of God as to whether he should fight and, if so, sought from him the nature of the attack (2 Sam. 5:17–25; 8:1).

It was common for the kings of Assyria, Babylonia, and Persia, like the Israelite kings, to call upon their prophets for oracles in their efforts to seek political resolutions or at least to determine the time and particulars of their own "pet" resolutions to political crises. Each king therefore had his own political prophets who were active strictly in the affairs of court. They did not speak directly to the people on the streets.

The prophets of Israel were different because they were raised up by God to exercise a corrective ministry as reminders, often opposing the kings by contending that God alone is the king of his people. Since the office of prophet was independent of kingship, often the prophets entered into open conflict with the monarchy. They continually exposed the peoples' and leaders' transgressions of the well-known commandments, for they were the ones who stressed the ethical demands of the religion of Israel. They appeared in public to deliver their messages using the traditional formula, "Thus says Yahweh." They were transmitting God's words to those to whom God sent them and to those who sought out the prophets for advice.

One of the greatest confrontations of spiritual powers recorded in the Bible took place during this period on Mt. Carmel when both Elijah and the prophets of Baal appealed to their respective deities (1 Kings 18:16–40). With all the people present Elijah challenged them, "If the Lord is God, worship him; if Baal is God, worship him!" The ocular demonstration followed as both Elijah and the prophets of Baal agreed that the god who sends down fire for the sacrifice will be God. With the people cheering, the prophets of Baal danced, prayed, and even cut themselves to attract their god, who remained silent. Elijah prepared the altar and the sacrifice and then had the people pour water over it. Then he prayed, "Prove now that you are God of Israel." The Lord sent fire down immediately. The people fell to the ground and corporately recognized the truth demonstrated in this power encounter — "The Lord is God; the Lord alone is God!"

This historical period with the presence of a king and a central place of worship produced great doxological statements that focused on God's power. David before a great assembly proclaims:

> Lord God of our ancestor Jacob, may you be praised for ever and ever! You are great and powerful, glorious, splendid, and majestic. Everything in heaven and earth is yours, and you are king, supreme ruler over all. All riches and wealth come from you; you rule everything by your strength and power; and you are able to make anyone great and strong. (1 Chron. 29:10–12)

In time of war the people of Judah came to the temple — "O Lord God of our ancestors, . . . you are powerful and mighty, and no one can oppose you. You are our God" (2 Chron. 20:6–7). In the Psalms God's power is often acknowledged (for example, Pss. 21:13; 68:33–35). As such great scriptural affirmations were repeated, the people were taught and reminded of the power of the great God who is their leader.

God's power is also shown in this period by his wrath, which was often aroused because of the disobedience of his people (2 Kings 17:13ff.; 22:17). He brought famine to their cities, killed their young men in battle, and sent locusts to eat the crops (Amos 4:6–12). Foreign invasion, destruction, disease, devastating fire — all are attributed to God's fierce anger (Isa. 9:8–10, 20).

The Exile

After several centuries of monarchy with the kings and Israelites failing to follow the laws of God, worshiping other gods, and defiling the temple, God's punishment came to his people with force in the fall of Jerusalem. The Israelites had been warned by Jeremiah, Ezekiel, and other prophets of the catastrophe that was to fall on the nation because of their idolatry and disobedience. They came to understand God's power more clearly when God in response to their ignoring him and his prophets' warnings of doom and destruction brought the king of Babylon to attack Jerusalem and conquer his people (2 Chron. 36:13–21). The temple was looted and destroyed, and many of the political and religious leaders were killed or carried off to Babylon to live in captivity. There they were made slaves and scattered so they were not able to be rebellious. Because of the limited power of Hebrew kingship and the reality of the Israelites' covenant-Lord relationship, the Lord enabled his people to survive the destruction of the kingdom.

When the temple feast and sacrificial worship had to be discontinued, new forms were needed. The departed Israelites became aware of their desperate need for something to hold fast to, some means of protecting themselves against their environment, something from which they could gain strength. Some of them found the law to be the answer. They reasoned that because the law had not been obeyed, disaster had overtaken them; if it was now obeyed, there was hope of deliverance. The law thereby became the fixed and immovable rock to which they could cling. Its requirements became the guide for human conduct, and the fulfillment of its requirements raised one's status. Keeping the Sabbath holy, circumcision, the complexity of dietary and purification laws, separation codes vis-à-vis non-Jews, and fasting in honor of God — all became very significant in this period.

A great power encounter in this period took place between Nebuchadnezzar and his god and the God of Daniel and his three friends. When Daniel's three friends in faithfulness and obedience to their God refused to bow down to a golden statue, they were thrown into a blazing furnace but were miraculously preserved (Daniel 3). On another occasion when Daniel spent the night unharmed in the midst of hungry lions, the king recognized the great power of Daniel's God. He sent word to the people throughout his empire commanding them to respect and fear Daniel's God who "is a living God, and will rule for ever" (Dan. 6:26). Georg Fohrer notes that this pattern of triumphant faith attracted people from other nations and religions, presumably deportees from other places living in the area, in such a way that they joined the Israelites (1972:312). What began to emerge, therefore, was a growing religious community rather than a purely racial entity as had existed prior to the exile.

The prophets of the exile, delivering their message in a particular context — the fabric of faith must be preserved! — often broadened their witness to include universal statements about the nature of God and his demands upon all peoples (Isa. 45:6; Jer. 23:23–24; Ezek. 33:11; Mal. 3:16–4:3). Several prophets spoke from God, revealing that he brings kings to power and also dethrones them (Dan. 2:21; 4:17; Jer. 27:6; Isa. 45:1–4). His sovereign control of the nations is more explicitly detailed than previously. Power belongs to God. No weapon forged by human being or Satan can withstand him or frustrate his will for his people.

NEW TESTAMENT ACTS SHOWING GOD'S POWER

In the first century c.e. the Roman Empire covered a multicultural area, and the gods of Hellenism had mixed in with many of the local religions. Astrology and magic were increasing in popularity. The major gods had followings of hosts of demons and lower spirits. The Romans had set up shrines in homes and at the crossroads for people to worship. Religion in this period was generally directed toward power, control, and wealth. Throughout the Hellenistic world the spirit world was seen to exercise influence over every aspect of life. Magicians were manipulating the spirits, both good and evil, in the interest of the individual person. Clinton Arnold, in his study of power and magic in the religious setting of the book of Ephesians, writes:

> Magical practices crossed all boundaries. "Magical" beliefs and practices can be found in the mystery cults and even in Judaism and Christianity. At this point it is essential to ask how one can differentiate between "religion" and "magic." ... In religion one prays and requests from the gods; in magic one commands the gods and therefore expects guaranteed results. (1989:18–19)

Belief in demons and a keen interest in supernatural power were characteristic of the first century.

Greek language and culture were dominant in this part of the world at this time. However, the outlook of the New Testament as a whole is prevailingly Jewish, and the New Testament as a group of documents is not expressive of the Greek or Roman mind. Its kinship is "primarily and overwhelmingly with Judaism and the Old Testament" (Filson 1950:26). Even though the Greek language was used for writing the New Testament, Hebrew concepts were being expressed.

In the New Testament the conflict between the forces of God and those of Satan comes into focus. Satan is seen as active and working to overthrow the purposes of God (1 Pet. 5:8, 9; 1 Tim. 3:7; 1 Thess. 2:18). Jesus refers to Satan as "the ruler of this world" (John 14:30), the one responsible for taking away the good seed sown in people's hearts (Mark 4:15), the cause of a woman's sickness (Luke 13:16).

Jesus believed in the reality of demonic forces and recognized them as personalities in their own right. The power of the kingdom of God became obvious as he defeated the spiritual enemies at work in the world. After his baptism, power and authority were predominant characteristics of his life. Satan challenged him and was defeated (Luke 4:1–12). Jesus became literally the extension of the power of God in the world. He ordered the evil spirits, and they responded (Luke 4:36; 6:18; Matt. 8:28–34); he forgave sins (Luke 5:24); he healed the sick (Mark 6:56); he raised the dead (Luke 8:54); he calmed the storm (Luke 8:22–25). When he sent the disciples out to speak, he gave them power over evil spirits, power to heal the sick and raise the dead (Matt. 10:6–8; Mark 6:7; Luke 9:1).

Jesus was obedient to God in allowing evil powers to crucify him. The power encounter of his death on the cross culminating in the victory of the resurrection won liberation for the people of God from their bondage to the power of Satan (Col. 2:14; Heb. 2:14, 15).

Pentecost then marked the filling of Christ's followers with power through their reception of the Holy Spirit (Acts 1:8). In turn they went out to do the mighty acts of God with the power not of humankind, but of God, who "raised up Christ from the dead." The signs and wonders done by the Spirit-filled apostles of Christ include casting out evil spirits, healing the sick, and raising the dead (Acts 3:1–4:22; 5:15, 16; 8:5–13; 9:32–43; 13:4–12; 16:16ff.; 20:7ff.; 28:8–9). As the people of God humbly obeyed Christ's command, God showed his power through the acts that were performed. At times the ones demonstrating God's power were put in jail, but another intervention of God's power set them free (Acts 3:1–4:22; 5:12–42; 16:16ff.). As a result of the wonders and miracles Stephen did, he was opposed by the leadership and taken before the council (Acts 6:8ff.). After presenting the gospel message in a powerful way, he was stoned to death. Only one conversion — that of Saul — is recorded as a result of Stephen's acts. However, in most cases where miracles were performed, either specific persons are named who believed afterward or the Scriptures state that many believed and the disciples were increasing in number (Acts 3:1–4:4; 5:12–16; 8:4–13; 13:4–12).

God had been doing miraculous work through Paul, healing people and driving out demons. As a result, unbelieving Jews tried to use Jesus' name to drive out evil spirits. The seven sons of the Jewish high priest, Sceva, when they misused Jesus' name, were overpowered by the man with the evil spirit (Acts 19:13–16). When word of this got around Ephesus, the people were filled with fear and recognized how great God's power was. Many believers responded by bringing their magic books and burning them in public. This along with the fight that the sons of Sceva lost provided ocular demonstration of God's power and resulted in the spreading of God's message and in many new believers.

During this historical period the tension between the kingdom of God introduced by Christ and the kingdom of Satan is made clear. This opposition between the two kingdoms is summarized in 2 Cor. 4:4, where Satan is seen to exercise his rule by holding human beings in darkness. Christ's death and resurrection defeated Satan and freed those who follow Christ from their bondage to Satan. The acts of God performed by Peter, Paul, and others spoke to the relevance of God to everyday life and to the power of the Holy Spirit.

GENERAL SUMMARY

There are a few observations to be made concerning the ideal and the real as they relate to spiritual power. It has been made very clear in Scripture that God is the power source (Ps. 62:11) and that he is capable and in touch with the needs for spiritual power that any people from any culture might have. He is the Creator of everything (Ps. 148:5) and the one who keeps life going (Ps. 65:5–8). Down through the ages he has chosen to work through the covenant relationship: he has promised great things, and he expects the obedience of his people. He depends on the people of God to be a witness to himself and a demonstration of the values of the kingdom (for example, justice, holiness, righteousness, service, peace, equality).

This is the ideal, but then, as has been obvious in this study, we have to deal with the actual or real, and not just reiterate the standards of the ideal. Due to human nature there will always be this difficulty. Some of the problems encountered in this study, actual things that have happened, have resulted from certain tendencies, including (1) looking to other human beings rather than to God for answers and hungering for the activity of any powers rather than turning solely to God; (2) being impatient with God's timing and hurrying ahead with one's own ideas; (3) failing to keep God and his acts clearly in mind and not staying close enough to God to seek his assistance. We have also seen much evidence of God's patience with human beings as they flounder, and also his firmness when they refuse to repent and obey.

My own understanding of spiritual power and how it relates to Christians, an understanding based on Scripture, is summarized as follows: (1) God and other spiritual powers, both good and evil, exist; (2) God is in ultimate control and the victory is his; (3) Satan and the evil powers are active in this world — he is the ruler of this world; (4) spiritual powers interact with and influence human beings, even shaping institutions; (5) human beings respond to spiritual powers sometimes consciously and at other times unconsciously; (6) God in his omniscience uses his power to make himself known to human beings, to show his love and concern for their needs, to demand a hearing, to punish and correct, and to give guidance; (7) Christ in his death and resurrection defeated Satan, making it possible for Christians to be free from the evil one; (8) God intends for his followers to be obedient to him and be an extension of his presence and power on earth; and (9) God has made available to his followers his power and authority in order that they might draw others to him and free people from the evil one.

The methods God has used as he worked with his people in covenant relationship are varied. He generally used that with which humans were already familiar — for example, language, sacrifice systems, a covenant system. When he used old forms, he deliberately put new meanings into them, as he did with the concepts of prophet and sacrifice. He began where his audience was and then gradually moved them to where he wanted them to be — for example, from "no other gods before me" to "other gods are not real gods." But everything he used from a given culture had its meaning centered in God himself. In many places Scripture illustrates how religious commitment takes only a relatively short time to develop, but dealing with magical practices and lifestyle changes takes a long time. As God's power is made real and allowed to operate in fullness, the need for other power sources declines. It is obvious that as God interacts with humans he is bringing about worldview changes.

God's power is never given merely to inflate the receptor. Obedience to him and depending on him in daily activities are of great importance. He wants his followers to be faithful and give his message to the world. God has not promised good health, comfortable living, and no trials. According to Scripture, power is safe only in the hands of God (2 Cor. 12). He is not to be controlled or manipulated by human beings. He is a God of power, the Creator and Controller of the universe, and he has promised to be faithful to his followers, providing for them as he sees fit.

PART III

GUIDES AND EXAMPLES

Chapter 7

Sample Case Studies

In this chapter I will compare the worldviews of three different societies as they relate to spiritual powers. My research showed that people in all of them were reaching out for spiritual power to meet similar felt needs. However, the worlds in which they lived were very different. There was variation in the definition of the spiritual world around them, the understanding of the possible causes for what happens in life, the person-group relationship, and the views of time and space. For a more thorough discussion of these case studies, see my dissertation, "Reaching Out for Spiritual Power: A Study in the Dynamics of Felt Needs and Spiritual Power" (1990).

The three groups I chose to research, work that included library research and field study, are the Navajo, the Thai, and the Kamwe. The Thai culture was chosen because of the longtime presence and importance of one of the world's great religions, Buddhism. It also represents a peasant society. The Navajo represent a tribal group that has survived many years of pressure from outside cultures. They also represent a pastoral society. The Kamwe represent a tribal group that, though under colonial rule for many years, was not forced to make many changes in their lifestyle. They are a horticultural society.

I approached this research recognizing that there is variation in world-view within each cultural group. This is due, in part, to the influence of formal schooling, military service, urbanization, modern media, and direct exposure to other societies. I have tried to represent the majority group in each geographical area.

INTRODUCING THE CASE STUDIES

A very brief history of each group will provide the backdrop for understanding the worldview that will be discussed later in the chapter.

The Navajo

The Navajos are the largest tribe of Native Americans in the United States today. Linguistically and culturally they are clearly a tribe, but they never functioned politically as a tribal unit until recent years with the formation of the Navajo Tribal Council. They are now called the Navajo Nation and have great pride in their identity and accomplishments.

Historically the Navajos were hunters and moved around in search of game and plant food. During the Spanish-American period (1630–1846) many important changes took place in their culture through raiding and trading contacts with the Spanish and also intensive contacts with the Pueblo Indians. Through Navajo raids against the Spanish they began to acquire domestic animals — horses, sheep, and goats. Maintaining peace proved to be difficult because treaties and agreements made with one Navajo took care of only the one small group over which he had political power.

By the end of this period, the Navajos practiced transhumance, moving their sheep into lower or higher altitudes at certain seasons. They were a multiresidence people as they pastured their sheep, with part of the family moving and part staying in one place. The men owned and herded the horses and went on raids. The women owned and herded most of the sheep (with the assistance of the children) and did the weaving.

In 1846, as a result of the Mexican War, the United States took over the Navajo area. The Navajos, independent and powerful, continued their raiding on the newcomers in the area. The American government sent expeditions against the Navajo to establish peace. Since Navajo settlement and political organization was so dispersed, raids continued even after peace treaties were agreed upon.

By 1863 the government decided to resettle the Navajo at Fort Sumner in order to teach them to build villages, learn to farm, and become "civilized" citizens of the United States. The Navajos were forced into captivity. The plan to change them into farmers failed for a variety of reasons, and in 1868 a treaty was drawn up allowing the Navajos to return to their homeland. The raiding complex was eliminated, and the Navajos were brought under the federal government. The reservation was established, and they were given a few sheep and goats, seeds and tools, as they arrived back in their homeland to start over again.

After the establishment of the reservation, contacts between Navajos and Anglos centered around Indian agents and the Indian service, the traders, and missionaries. The main goal of the government was to help the Navajos recover economically and then educate them as quickly as possible into American culture. The government called on the church to send missionaries to help in this task.

Ruth Underhill writes of these early years of reservation life:

> To the credit of the Navajos is the fact that during this period of stress, they had never ceased to do their part in working toward self-support. In 1871, the commissioner's report stated, "The Navajo are a hard working people and but for their unfortunate location, they might have been self-sustaining by this time...." In 1878: "They have grown from a band of paupers to a nation of prosperous, industrious, shrewd and intelligent people." (1956:175)

The Navajo herds increased until they were as large as in ancient raiding days. The population increased also, and the reservation was extended from time to time. But at no time did the growth of the reservation keep pace with the growth of the population.

In the 1930s a stock reduction program was planned by the government to bring the number of livestock in line with the amount of grazing land in order to stop soil erosion. To the Navajos livestock was a sign of the blessing and provision of the spiritual powers and was tied closely to their religious activity. Furthermore, social status was determined largely by the amount of livestock the family owned. The program was enforced in spite of the Navajo opposition.

The Navajo Tribal Council was established to speak for the tribe when oil was discovered on the reservation. By 1948 it became an elected, representative body that is largely responsible for tribal affairs.

Peyotism or the Native American Church is popular on the reservation today. It began in the 1930s through contacts with another Indian tribe. In the early days there was much opposition from traditional religionists, Christians, and the U.S. government. It was not until 1967 that the Native American Church won legal rights in tribal law, allowing members to transport Peyote into Navajo country and buy, sell, possess, and use Peyote in connection with the religious practices, sacraments, and services of the church.

Peyotism was attractive to the Navajo in that it clearly rejected assimilation and acculturation, which were being pushed on them. Deprivation of power on top of deprivation of possessions, status, and worth (brought on by the stock reduction) opened the door for the Peyote religion. Peyote was often viewed as a way to expand power: whereas in Navajo traditional religion the powers operated only in Navajoland, the power offered by Peyote could be seen as operating everywhere.

The Thai

The Thai kingdom had its beginning in the thirteenth century. Wars with neighboring Cambodia, Laos, and Burma caused the borders to contract and expand. Also for nearly three hundred years there was almost incessant internal strife among the small rival kingdoms. In the eighteenth century a religious monarchical system was established with the capital in Bangkok. Thailand has since became a strong centralized state, a major power in Southeast Asia.

In 1932, however, a coup d'état, organized by a small middle-class group, was completely successful, placing members of the royal family under house arrest. At this time a constitutional monarchy was set up in place of the previous absolute monarchy. From that time until the present the position of the king has been regarded as being above politics. However, in the villagers' eyes, the king embodies the merit believed necessary in one who rules, and thus he symbolically confers the right to rule on his ministers.

Today Thailand is the only surviving monarchy in Southeast Asia. It was able to remain independent even during the expansion of the West when the Chinese empires and the kingdoms of Burma, Cambodia, and Annam succumbed. The Thai monarchs in the nineteenth century proved to be masters of diplomacy with a policy of being friends of all and enemies of none. They also found it necessary to undertake political, social, and cultural changes within the country in order to maintain the independence of the kingdom. Since Thailand was economically a client state of Great Britain for most of the first half of this century, Great Britain has had much influence on development there, especially in economics. The wealth of Thailand is in its agriculture, with over 80 percent of its people living in the rural areas. The kin group controls the land — either the household group or a collection of households bound together by proximity and by kinship.

Phya Anuman Rajadhon, an eminent Thai scholar, comments on the focus of Thai culture:

> Fundamentally, the culture of Thailand may be summed up in one word, religion. For everything, art and literature, social system, habits and customs, is developed and clustered around her religion. (1968:23)

Animism, with ancestor worship, is the primitive belief of the Thai. Later on from Ceylon came Buddhism, which became the national religion when the Thai kingdom was formed. Also the Thai inherited many Hindu (Brahman) forms and concepts through Cambodia. James Gustafson explains how the roles of each of these three traditions affect the life of the Thai peasant (1970:78): Theravada Buddhism is the basis of the moral system; animism is the basis of the daily life routine; Brahmanism is the basis for life-cycle ceremonies; and both animism and Brahmanism provide the basis for the Thai beliefs in gods and spirits.

Reincarnation as taught in Theravada Buddhism is a part of Thai worldview. However, in all Theravada Buddhist societies those who are actually aspiring to becoming fully enlightened are very rare. Nirvana for most is a very remote goal that can be achieved only after many existences. An alternative religious goal is provided by the law of karma, which says that suffering can be reduced by meritorious actions and avoiding demeritorious actions. The wisdom of the Buddha says:

> Wherein does religion consist? It consists in doing as little harm as possible, in doing good in abundance, in the practice of love, of compassion, or truthfulness and purity, in all walks of life. (Shipp 1946:7)

Merit making is not done to influence a divine or secular authority but as a personal concern, privilege, and obligation to oneself. Belief in reincarnation places the responsibility on the individual to better him/herself. Since women are not allowed to gain merit by being a novice or a monk, they are more conscientious about interacting daily with the monks. The older men, as they approach the end of life, are naturally more interested in gaining merit.

One very clear Brahman concept that has been taken over by the Thai is divine kingship. Though the country is no longer ruled by an absolute monarch, there is still a sacred aura about the king. For the Thai, Brahmanism has supplied a whole pantheon of gods and goddesses and the religious offerings of candles, incense sticks, and flowers. Also the concept of a soul-spirit that resides in each human being is Brahman.

From animism the Thai have the concept of the atmosphere and surroundings being full of autonomous spirit powers that affect daily living. These powers can assist a person if treated well or harm one if they are overlooked, insulted, or abused.

The Kamwe

The Kamwe, a tribal group (about three hundred thousand) living primarily in the hilly area in northeastern Nigeria, are one of the many small, isolated tribes in what is called the Middle Belt, although they also spill over into the Cameroon Republic. They have been called "Higi" (meaning aborigine) by outsiders and in written materials, but they refer to themselves as Kamwe, "the people of the mountain." Recent historians have traced the origin of the Kamwe to the Kingdom of Kush, which was situated between present Egypt, Sudan, and Ethiopia. From there they moved to what is presently the Central African Republic area, then on to the Cameroons, then to Nigeria.

Politically they have never functioned as a unit, though they clearly are linguistically and culturally unified. Each village was settled by one or two clans with its own chief and elders, independent of all others. C. K. Meek once observed that villagers viewed other villagers as enemies unless they used the same water supplies and market (1931:253).

The Kamwe practice for the most part subsistence agriculture, though their social structure includes one caste of craftsmen who trade goods and services for some of their food. Royalty exists in both the agricultural and crafts castes. Marriage must be within one's own caste.

The unit of government before colonialism was the patrilineal kindred, with several kindreds forming the local group. Each group recognized the spiritual authority of the local chief. He did not have executive power but was powerful in his spiritual responsibility for successful harvests and the welfare of the people. The chief, whose position was inherited, was an adviser and an arbiter on all important matters.

Fulani pastoralists migrated to this same area, and at first they lived peacefully. Later in the nineteenth century they became a threat to the cultural identity of the Kamwe and neighboring tribes. When the Fulani attempted to rule the Kamwe, the Kamwe were expected to pay tribute and donate labor. The Fulanis, who fought on horseback, were at a disadvantage in trying to control the Kamwe, as they were not able to negotiate the hills where the Kamwe lived and/or fled for safety.

In the twentieth century the Kamwe were made submissive first to German then to British colonial administrations. They were urged to move down from the hills and guaranteed safety. The majority of the Kamwe today inhabit the valleys, with many tending to maintain their homes close to the bases of the hills. After World War I the British, in taking charge of the area, set up "indirect rule," giving political power to the Fulani rulers in the area as they made them the district heads. This put the Kamwe in an awkward position since they had never been conquered by the Fulani:

It wasn't until 1936 when the Kamwe Native Court was formed that the Kamwe started to enjoy political rights and to feel like real citizens. The first Native Court was made up of five Kamwe chiefs, their five assistants and three lesser chiefs. By the late 1950s there were fifty qualified Kamwe chiefs who had the right to join the Native Court. (M. Kraft 1978:19)

A few Kamwe were elected to higher government positions (the House of Representatives in Lagos and the Kaduna House of Chiefs). Nigerian independence in 1960 opened up more government positions to the Kamwe.

Traders and government workers had passed through the area, but missionaries, arriving in 1957, were the first outsiders to live in the Kamwe area. As the roads have improved into the larger villages and towns in the Kamwe area, so has meaningful interaction with the outside world. This has also brought about a flow of Kamwe to and from the larger cities outside of their own geographical area.

The majority of Kamwe still follow their traditional religion. Belief in God, Hyalatamwe, who created everything and is kind, but who has gone far away because of humankind's carelessness, is central to their religion. Evil spirits, however, are the troublemakers and demand much more attention. The Kamwe are very conscious of the participation of spirits, including the ancestor spirits, in everyday activities.

Islam was brought into the Kamwe area by the Fulani. Because of the Fulani conquests and the threat of enslavement, the Kamwe as a group have not been attracted to converting to Islam. Christianity was brought into the area by some Kamwe men who had gone to a leprosarium operated by a mission. They stayed there for treatment until medication made it possible to arrest the disease and allow the patients to return home. They had become Christians. When they came home they told others of their relationship to God, and the people listened and many responded.

SIMILARITIES AND DISSIMILARITIES

All three groups are basically rural populations. However, they are dissimilar in that the Navajo are a pastoral society, the Thai a peasant society, and the Kamwe a horticultural society.

The Navajo had the matriarchal extended family as the basic social organization. The territorial group, the camp, centered around this unit with mother, daughters and their husbands, and granddaughters and their husbands tending to live in the same area. Economic factors related to herding and other activities affected the size of the camp. The camp was also the basic political unit, which mobilized with the other camps of the clan when necessary.

The Thai are basically a peasant society with weak leadership patterns in the village and little independence. Governed by a few elite Thai, the peasants are in a subordinate relationship and feel powerless in the society. Agriculture, their means of livelihood, ties them in with the market towns and fluctuating prices, since a significant amount of what they produce is sold.

The Kamwe are a horticultural society practicing slash-and-burn agriculture. Their basic social organization is the patriarchal extended family. Until this century the Kamwe were an independent tribe with the extended family being the basic political unit and the patriarch the ascribed leader. They had a subsistence economy, producing all or most of their food and other needs.

Outside influence has been greater for the Navajo than it has for the other two societies. The Navajo underwent forced change when the U.S. government moved into their land. This involved moving them off their land for a few years, forcing children into school, forcing families to take the father's name as a surname, killing their herds and their horses. These incomprehensible events shook the core values of land, herd, family, and religion. The Thai have never been under colonial rule. Changes have come about through the choice and control of the ruling elite. The Kamwe were isolated, and when colonization occurred, the British allowed local leaders and courts to continue functioning.

The Navajo, in response to deprivations of land and herds and in their struggle for power against the federal government forces, opened up to Peyotism, which included a spiritual power broader than the reservation area. Since Christianity was a part of early government control, it was not popular. The Thai, though following Buddhism, continued their animistic beliefs and practices to meet daily needs. Christianity was not attractive to them. The Kamwe in their openness to Westernization in recent years have responded positively to Christianity and, due to early intertribal tensions, unfavorably to Islam.

SPIRITUAL POWER IN THREE SOCIETIES

Worldview concepts relating to spiritual power are distinct in these three societies. The fundamental assumptions about the nature of reality as it relates to spiritual power will be listed below for each society.

In the Navajo Worldview

The Navajos' central concern is unity in the spirit realm. This generates a feeling of understanding, concern, peace, and identity with the surroundings — in nature, people, animals. Everything was brought into being in perfect harmony, so when disharmony arises (sickness, misfortune, strained relationships) the challenge is to go back to the original order. Since the four cardinal directions were carefully put in place in the beginning and since there is special power in each of the mountains in those directions, it is natural that ceremonies to restore harmony focus on the four directions and that four has become an auspicious number. Curing ceremonies involve formal recitation of the origins by a specialist, with right order being very significant. To restore harmony it is necessary to diffuse evil powers and bring good powers. In ritual the power moves from the center outward, with those at the center receiving most, but all who attend receiving some.

Another Navajo assumption is the importance of the individual. Though each person has a part of the spirit world within, it is necessary to open up to more spiritual powers, for this is what makes humans different from animals. As people participate in the spiritual world they derive power for living. Individuals choose which kind of spiritual power (good or evil) they let in and use, therefore being responsible for their own place in life. It is thought that choosing evil influences reveals a weak spirit within. One's spirit can be weak, but it does not leave the body until death, when it normally dissolves in the spirit world. Humans can misuse power, and this results in witchcraft and sorcery. A person's relationship to others and to the spirit world is characterized by reciprocity. The individual has the right to decide what to share and what to do, and if one helps others and is responsible with what has been given (for example, sheep, food) by the spirit world, one will receive accordingly.

Another basic assumption is that death is dangerous and attracts evil spirit activity. Those who practice witchcraft often use parts of a corpse in their practice. With no clear belief in an afterworld, Navajos believe that there is always the possibility that the spirit within a person will become a harmful ghost at death, especially if death is premature. The burial ceremony is simple, and only a few family members participate.

Navajos also assume that some things are inherently good and others inherently evil. Corn pollen, which is sacred and good, attracts good spiritual power and is used in both formal and informal rituals. Lightning, being evil, destroys and brings evil to whatever it strikes. It upsets the harmony and requires a ceremony for restoration.

Another basic assumption is that protection from evil spirit activity (witchcraft, sorcery, unknown spirits) is found in curing ceremonies where good spirit power is used to put things back in harmony. Protection is also found in amulets that contain corn pollen and other items used in personal interaction with the spiritual.

In the Thai Worldview

One of the most evident assumptions in Thai supernaturalism is that reality includes a great variety of active spirits with which one must deal. Each geographical area, each business, and each piece of private property has a spirit associated with it, and a house is constructed for the spirit outside each building but somewhere on the property. Inside the home an ancestor shelf and often a Buddha shelf are found. These spirits can cause trouble if they are not cared for and respected. The Thai are conscious of the need to be in good standing with these spirits, and they also see that there is spiritual power available to them if they need it. Candles, incense, food, and/or flowers are commonly placed in a variety of places to gain favor from the spirits — on the ancestor shelf, in the household spirit house, on the Buddha shelf, in the village shrine, in the temple, and in other shrines set up for various spirits. There are also capricious spirits who attack one unawares, and they need to be discovered and dealt with. Benevolent gods and goddesses provide another spiritual source for assistance in daily life. The rice goddess and the sacredness of rice require special ceremonies at various times in the development and use of rice.

Thais also believe in the existence of the soul-spirit, who lives in each human being and is essential for health and life. Special soul-tying ceremonies are needed for life cycle and other changes so that the soul-spirit remains in the body.

Another assumption in Thai worldview is that individuals are responsible for their own status in life. This involves the merit one enters the world with, the merit accumulated throughout life by having the merit outweigh the demerits, and the merit gained through another's efforts (for example, at a funeral). Getting into the afterlife in good shape so one can be reborn at a higher level in society requires an elaborate and careful death ritual. Death attracts evil spirits, and there is always the chance that the spirit of the dead person will escape.

Thais believe that following Buddhist values and practices will bring rewards for the present life. This includes the deep respect that is shown to elders, monks, and the king; servicing the monks; joining the monkhood for a period of time; and visiting the temple. Pali scripts, the Buddha image, and auspicious numbers (uneven ones and especially nine) are often used in making amulets that are used for protection, especially in unfamiliar and unpredictable territory. Pali scripts have power in themselves and are recited not only by the monks in a great variety of ceremonies but also by spirit doctors and elders who preside over ceremonies. Holy water that has been blessed by the monks is used in Buddhist and other rituals.

Another assumption of the Thai is the belief that the spirit of a deceased person or of a village shrine or of a specific area does enter a person when it is invited to give assistance and deal with a problem. Many people go to the spirit mediums for spiritual insight and instruction for their various problems.

In the Kamwe Worldview

The basic assumption of Kamwe supernaturalism is that all spiritual power issues from a single source, God the creator. God is ultimately in control and is just. Joseph Takwale writes of the Kamwe perception of God as the one who

> created everything perfect with no sickness and no death. People were fed on a cloud God made which hung over the blue mountain within reach of the people. When people became careless and broke some of God's rules God moved his home skyward, slowly out of the reach of the people. Then trouble, sickness and death came. (1967)

God is seen as far away and not much involved in daily activities.

The Kamwe have a hierarchical system with God at the top, then his ambassadors, including both good and evil spirits, then the ancestor spirits, who are closer to human beings. Good spirits do not cause trouble, so the ones to look out for are the evil spirits. These spirits reside in specific areas — in trees, rivers, stones, mountains, and caves — known to the people, who observe taboos in those areas. Spirits may appear in the form of very old men, big snakes, tiny babies, or white mice. Care must be taken not to offend these spirits. Seeing a spirit may result in blessing or misfortune. Only one type of spirit can possess a person, and that spirit is inherited through the maternal line. This spirit stays with a person throughout life. It is usually thought of as evil, but it can be used for good by the person who is possessed.

The ancestor spirits are the ones who understand humans best because they were once human beings. The ancestors are regarded as part of the living family, but they live in the afterworld. Another assumption of the Kamwe is that the ancestors need assistance from those on earth, and those on earth need assistance from the ancestors. This involves a very deep respect and honor for elders in the society and also a fear of being cursed by an elder. Death ceremonies are very important to the whole family because one needs to get the spirit safely settled with those who have gone before.

Another Kamwe assumption is that the spiritual plays a role in both the good things and the unfortunate things that happen. Sickness and misfortune can be caused by offending a spirit, being cursed by an elder for breaking the standards of the family, offending ancestors by failing to follow their teaching and values, breaking the taboos of society (which brings punishment by spiritual powers), witchcraft, or sorcery. The elder may go to a diviner to discover the specific cause. The diviner can identify the thief, the adulterer, the offended spirit, the cause of death, or whatever the problem is.

The Kamwes also believe that both good and evil are ultimately in the hands of God. This brings about an accepting attitude toward life. Human beings try to live peaceably and work out problems, but justice will be brought about by God himself.

Another assumption is that the individual's identity is in the extended family. Family members carry a great responsibility for one another. One gives and one receives from this very tight unit. When one does not spend time with others, he/she is suspected of witchcraft or sorcery. A female leaves her family of birth and joins her husband's family. It is important to be buried with the family in the burial grounds on the mountain of origin.

The Kamwe also believe that spiritual power is found in high places and in guinea corn. The mountain signifies a closeness to God and more power. Guinea corn, a gift of God, is used to give strength to the people and for effective interaction with spiritual powers and other human beings.

In conclusion, we have seen how the world of spiritual power varies in these three societies. Even though protective amulets are used in all of them, the items used, the way they are made powerful, and the occasion for their use vary. Though the basic needs for spiritual power are similar, the beliefs concerning what powers are available and how to obtain power are different. Understanding worldview helps one feel like an insider and provides the foundation for relevant communication of the gospel.

Chapter 8

Investigating Supernaturalism

Worldview is difficult to uncover since it is comprised of the deep-level assumptions, values, and commitments held by a society and is learned for the most part unconsciously. One way to understand worldview is to describe the themes and counterthemes within a culture. Morris Opler notes the importance of these themes:

A limited number of dynamic affirmations...can be identified in every culture and the key to the character, structure, and direction of the specific culture is to be sought in the nature, expression, and interrelationship of these themes. (Opler 1946:198)

Themes tend to control behavior and stimulate activity as approved by society. Focusing on traits and themes relating to the spiritual will provide an understanding of the dynamics of the society. Themes, which permeate all areas of culture, make equilibrium possible.

The influence of Greek dualism on our concept of the supernatural leads toward a perspective that separates the natural from the supernatural. However, I have chosen to use the term "supernaturalism" to label the cultural theme found in the worldviews of societies where there is a primary concern with spirits and the spiritual realm. The common theme of supernaturalism was found in Navajo, Thai, and Kamwe worldviews. Each of these societies has the basic assumption that spiritual power is available to human beings. It is necessary for success, guidance, giving order to the universe, and meeting crises such as illness, accident, barrenness, and drought. People in each of these societies have committed themselves to working with spiritual powers in culturally prescribed ways.

Investigating the present beliefs that underlie behavior makes it possible to define the felt needs for spiritual power that need to be met and dealt with in the framework of Christianity.

UNIVERSALS OF WORLDVIEW

Four universals of worldview that help in the collecting and organizing of data are: (1) classification, (2) the person-group relation, (3) causality, and (4) the perception of time and space. Each of these can be investigated in relation to spiritual powers. I will illustrate with examples from the case studies.

Classification in Relation to Spiritual Power

Classification of spiritual powers is the way people categorize them (for example, gods and goddesses, ancestor spirits, malevolent spirits, guardian spirits), how/if they distinguish between supernatural and natural, the arrangement of the spiritual powers (for example, hierarchical, geographical), and the interrelationship of each group with human beings. For instance, to the Navajo lightning is always an evil spirit power, and when one comes in contact with it a curing ceremony is required. An interviewee explained how when she was eight years old she was bringing about fifteen sheep into the corral when lightning struck the sheep just a few feet from her. She kicked the sheep to see if they would get up. Her family told her she shouldn't have done that, and they made her stay in the pasture with the dead sheep. The medicine man was contacted for a curing ceremony that was then held in the pasture for her and the sheep.

Among the Thai the concept of a spirit working through a medium, one who has agreed to allow the spirit to use his/her body in order to provide services for patients, is widespread. A guardian spirit or the spirit of a dead person may coerce the person through threat of illness or death or through a promise to heal the person from a sickness if he/she agrees. The medium is responsible to regularly place food and other things desirable to the spirit on the spirit shelf constructed for the spirit in his/her home. The spirit only possesses the person when invited, however.

The Kamwe believe ancestor spirits entice the very sick person to join them through death. Very sharp thorns may be placed a few inches away from the sick person's head in order to harm the spirits of the dead who come at night trying to convince the patient to join them. An interviewee remembered being sent to the burial grounds to keep his sick sister's soul from joining the ancestor spirits there. He threw stones in every direction to prevent the soul from coming. The next day the sister was better, and his family was grateful for the good job he did preventing the soul from passing.

The Person-Group Relation and Spiritual Power

Definition of the relation between the person and the group is a part of every worldview. The place of spiritual power and its relationship to the person/group vary from society to society. The Navajo hold reciprocity as very important among clan members. Every debt must be repaid, and the ledger of obligations and favors received should remain in balance. Human beings have been given land, livestock, water, and farming by the spirit world, and in return they must care for what has been received. The Navajo individual can seek and use spiritual power by him/herself, or it may be a corporate experience as the group shares its oneness, striving to meet the needs of the individual.

A Thai person is taught early the importance of respect and a consciousness of knowing one's place in society. Respect must be shown to the king, Buddha, monks and novices, and all who are more advanced in age. Special classifiers in the language are used for the king, Buddha images, and monks (M. Kraft 1990:139). There is an underlying idea of mutual dependence — being practically and morally indebted with the recognition of the need for each other. Instructions for morality given in public school include the following:

- Do not try to act in the same way as your superior.

- Do not be concerned with your own comfort before the comfort of your superiors or women.

- If you are a superior, wherever you go, you should look after the comfort of your inferior. (Phillips 1966:44)

Respect also relates to the spirit realm. Skilled artisans and performers, such as the bronze casters and boxers, express their respect before a performance to their teachers and, behind the immediate teachers, to the spirit masters of their professions. They are seen as the "owners" of the art and the giver or withholder of successes in it.

For the Kamwe the individual has no identity apart from the group. John V. Taylor likens the relationship to the glow of a coal that depends on its remaining in the fire: "So the vitality, the psychic serenity, the very humanity of man, depends on his integration into the family" (1963:99). Because of the hierarchical arrangement of spiritual powers, the ancestors are closest to the family, and the older members of the family are closest to becoming ancestors. It is very important that they are respected. Therefore, it is very serious and even dangerous to disagree with an elder, because he/she may place a curse on a person that could cause barrenness, death of children, illness, or death.

Causality in Relation to Spiritual Power

Causality deals with what forces are at work in the universe. Cause and effect may involve powers in the natural world, human power, or spiritual power. Different societies pay different amounts of attention to these various areas.

For the Navajo proper relationship to everything in one's environment is important because of their central focus on harmony. Disharmony may be caused by witchcraft or sorcery (which involve using spiritual power against someone), ghost contact, breaking a taboo, or interpersonal problems.

For the Thai illness and misfortune are often perceived as having a spiritual cause: failure to show respect and honor to the ancestors, gods and goddesses, or guardian spirits; allowing the *khwan* spirit to escape from the body; offending the ancestors or guardian spirits; or the desire of the spirit of a dead person to possess a living person.

Causality for the Kamwe is centered on the spiritual. Both the good things and the bad things that happen in life are in the hands of the spirit world. Sickness and misfortune may be caused by offending a spirit or an ancestor spirit, being cursed by an elder, breaking a taboo, or witchcraft. If needed, diviners in the society are available to discover the specific cause and give advice as to how to remedy it.

Time-Space Perceptions in Relation to Spiritual Power

How time and space are perceived affects working with the spiritual. The appropriate time and place for meeting the spiritual, the arrangement of people to interact most effectively with spiritual powers, the flow of spiritual power, and use of objects with spiritual power are all part of the basic assumptions of a society and affect the behavior of the people.

For the Navajo corn pollen has special power. It is one of the essentials in the universe and is called mother, representing life and fertility. It is used in many ways in the curing chant: with prayer sticks as offering to spiritual beings, sprinkled ceremonially over a sand painting before the patient takes his place, to mark paths for the spirits, to dry with for the ceremonial bath at the end of a chant, and so on. It is also used often with private prayers, sprinkling it in the four directions. Pollen stands for peace, happiness, and all that is desirable and outside of conflict.

For the Thai, odd numbers are auspicious. An odd number of monks are invited for all rituals except the death ritual; an odd number of Pali scripts are repeated in rituals; and odd numbers are used on holy cloth. Since the realm of the dead is seen as inverted to the ordinary world, an even number of monks preside at the death ritual, and a little four-rung ladder is placed in the coffin to enable the spirit of the dead to escape. Monks, knowing the auspicious times of power often through astrology, are called on to set the date/time for special occasions, for example, opening a new business, a marriage, a funeral, and setting the location for a new spirit house. Monks can also infuse spirit power into water, Buddha images, amulets, and tattoos.

The mountain has special meaning to the Kamwe. Different clans settled on different mountains, so the ancestors are identified with specific mountains, and burial grounds are usually on the mountains. Often now the corpse has to be carried a distance to the burial grounds so that one can move on from this world with the clan. Originally compounds were located on the mountainside. The men and granaries were located on the higher side, and the downside was where the women lived and worked. This showed the hierarchy found in the society, placing the men in a position closer to God and his power. It also gave men the advantage in being able to see the enemy as they approached, so they could protect the compound. The Kamwe language shows the importance of the mountain in the common concept of "come and go," which requires one of eight specific relation-to-the-mountain terms (M. Kraft 1978:31–34). Locational prepositions also reflect this mountain orientation.

INTERVIEWING

One of the ways to learn about spiritual power as understood in another culture is interviewing. When interviewing it is good to meet the person where he/she feels most comfortable. Oftentimes my interviewing took place in the person's home, farm, or office, but on some occasions it was at the library, a restaurant, or at my place of lodging. The following questions provided insight for understanding worldview:

A. What are the spiritual powers available to help human beings?

 1. Is there one source of all spiritual power?

 2. Are some spiritual powers more powerful than others?

 3. Are there some spiritual powers that are always good and some that are always evil?

 4. Are there enemy spirit powers and friendly spirit powers?

 5. Are spirits/gods usually male or female?

 6. Are there spirit powers associated with geographical areas?

 7. Are there spirits/gods that need to be recognized regularly?

 8. Do women have the same access to spiritual power that men have?

B. What particular needs cause one to seek assistance from spiritual powers?

    1. When does one seek out spiritual power?

    2. Are the particular needs related to a particular spiritual power?

C. What spiritual powers are feared?

    1. How does one get protection?

    2. How does one obtain spiritual power?

D. Are there practitioners who deal directly with spiritual power?

    1. What kinds of practitioners?

    2. How does one decide which practitioner to go to?

    3. Who approaches the practitioner?

    4. Where do the practitioners get their power and knowledge?

    5. How are the practitioners paid for their services?

    6. Are the practitioners male or female?

E. Are there objects that have special spiritual power?

    1. Is the power inherent in the object, or has someone placed power in that object?

    2. On what occasions are these objects used?

    3. How are they used?

F. What ceremony/ritual is performed to gain spiritual power?

    1. Who is present?

    2. Where is it held?

    3. Who is in charge?

    4. When is it performed?

    5. Is there recognition of a spiritual power associated with mealtime?

    6. Can one speak directly with the spiritual power?

    7. What paraphernalia is used?

These questions provided a springboard for getting into much more detail in each of the societies. Often I was given examples/stories of how interaction with spiritual powers really took place on a specific occasion. Then I had the opportunity to ask related questions to gain further information and check the other answers that had been given.

    It is my hope that these ideas for discovering assumptions and values concerning spiritual power will give understanding and provide a springboard for further research. It is my intent to assist in developing the ability to look at life through someone else's lens in order to better understand needs and behavior.

DANGERS IN FOCUSING ON SPIRITUAL POWER

Since this kind of investigation has not traditionally been done as part of mission work, fear has been expressed concerning putting this much emphasis on pre-Christian views of spiritual power. As has been discussed throughout this book, understanding the assumptions, values, commitments, and needs of the receptors makes it possible to meet them where they are, communicating the gospel without so much interference. It also paves the way for ministering to the whole person, including the spiritual power needs, and opens the door for more relevant and meaningful ritual within the church. In this section I will discuss some of the dangers that some Christians have expressed regarding focusing on spiritual power and opening the church up to a more conscious involvement with the power of the Holy Spirit.

1. *Due to the nature of our humanness, seeking after spiritual power can easily become an ego trip.* This is more apt to be a problem in Western society with its emphasis on individualism than in the rest of the world. Calling on spiritual powers to meet personal felt needs is not the same as manipulating those around you so that you can exert control over them and be powerful in their eyes. The Bible clearly states that the works the Father does in us in Jesus' name are done so that "the Father may be glorified" (John 14:12–13). Whenever self-glorification takes place, it is clearly misuse of God's power. Love for those we serve is basic and will influence how spiritual power is used (John 13:34, 35). As we make ourselves available to be used by God, his power flows through us to help others. We are his stewards. Jesus modeled for us servanthood and humility (Phil. 2:7, 8).

The fear is that in a spiritual-power–oriented society the power Christians have in the Holy Spirit may be used as a replacement for magic in their pre-Christian experience. In practicing magic, human beings are manipulating spiritual power. Christians, however, are in submission to God and must accept what God wants to do through them. God is in control, and in no way should we try to manipulate him.

2. *Emphasizing and practicing God's power can easily become an end in itself.* Jesus lived and taught a balanced approach, emphasizing that salvation is more important than using God's power to control evil spirits (Luke 10:17–20). Power demonstrations and miracles were withheld when the Pharisees requested them of Jesus (Matt. 12:39; 16:4; Mark 8:11, 12). Never did Jesus perform miracles to be sensational. Demonstration of God's power as we see it in Scripture is definitely a means to an end — drawing people closer

to God himself, with conversion being the focus (Matt. 15:30, 31; 20:34; Mark 10:52; Luke 5:25; 18:43; John 4:53; 11:45).

It is interesting that public Christian healing meetings often draw large crowds who are interested in bettering their situation. Some are drawn closer to God and a fuller understanding of who he is, and others get healed and go on their way without any turning to God. It is like the situation of the lepers Jesus healed as recorded in Luke 17:12–19. However, many times in mission work a neighbor's or friend's prayer for a sick person who is non-Christian has resulted in God showing his healing power, and this leads to faith in God.

3. *There is a danger in divorcing spiritual power from truth.* Being preoccupied with miracles may cause neglect of studying God's Word, where truth is found. Sin, justice, divine judgment, social responsibility, righteousness, and peace are all important in Scripture and must be dealt with as part of the truth of God. The crucifixion of Christ, Christ as the power of God, *and* the wisdom of God are all emphasized in 1 Cor. 1:23–24. Care must be taken to deal with both power *and* wisdom.

Spiritual power is only one part of Christian living. It may be a more important part to those of other cultures than it is to the Westerner. However, in order to be obedient to God, it is necessary to follow his instructions in his Word. On the other hand, a legalistic following of the Word without the love of Christ is useless (1 Cor. 13). To study God's Word with the Holy Spirit as teacher within us will bring balance in our lives and prepare us to use the power God has given for his honor and glory.

4. *Confusion may result in recognizing what power is from God and what is from the evil one.* Since using spiritual power for human benefit is common to many different societies and religions today, it is crucial to be alert and actively discern what is from God and what is not (1 John 4:1–6). If the name "Jesus" is being used, we must be sure that the power being referred to is not just one created in human thought or one that is evil. It must refer to the incarnate Christ if it is of God. God's power is evidenced through the working of the Holy Spirit in his followers. Christ is the center for Christians, and daily living will give evidence of the fruit of God's Spirit (Gal. 5:22, 23). According to 1 Cor. 12:3, acknowledging the lordship of Christ can be done only by the Holy Spirit's presence. So investigating the relationship of the practitioner to Christ would reveal whether the power being used is of God. Anything that happens that is contradictory to the teachings of Christ and the Word of God is not of God.

5. *Focusing on felt needs and the power of the Holy Spirit may lead one to live under the lordship of emotions rather than the lordship of Christ.* Experiencing and feeling are important parts of Christianity. It is good to be able to feel and experience God's presence and guidance. However, the written Word of God was given us so that we might know what is right and wrong,

and it is necessary to be obedient to that Word and constantly acknowledge Christ as Lord. Such an obedience will result in a commitment to others, in an awareness of being the "Bible" others read, and in our being an expression of God's love and blessing to those around us. Lack of discipline may allow personal emotions to shift our focus and activity toward self-comfort, self-fulfillment, and self-glory. Personal discipline is required for constant study of God's Word, using it as a yardstick that measures how we are following God's will and heart. Our whole being is saying both intellectually and with our emotions, "He is Lord!"

The incarnated Christ was a great example of the importance of relationship both with the Father and with those Christ came to serve. He was very sensitive to doing what the Father wanted (John 5:19, 20; 8:28; 17:7, 8), and he also had great sensitivity to the needs of those around him.

In conclusion, care must be taken to not overemphasize spiritual power. Jesus' response to the seventy who returned with excitement over God's using them to curb Satan's activity was: "Nevertheless, do not rejoice in this, that the spirits are subject to you, but rejoice that your names are recorded in heaven" (Luke 10:17–20). Salvation is far more important than confrontation of the powers. There needs to be a balanced approach with Christ and the Scriptures as central. However, when we see how dependent on spiritual power so many of the societies of the world are, we must respond by promoting the God of Christianity as the one who has the power to do far beyond what we can imagine.

Chapter 9

Modernization and Concepts of Spiritual Power

We have examined the spiritual-power system in three different societies. Investigating worldview gives a general picture of the deep structure of society at a particular point in time. In this chapter the focus is on understanding the modernization process and what happens to spiritual-power beliefs when modernization takes place. Since the West over a period of many years turned from belief in the spiritual to belief in science, it is often assumed that the same transition takes place in other parts of the world when they take on new technology. However, anthropologists have observed that worldview, which is at the center of culture, changes much more slowly than such things as technology, lifestyle, or addition of artifacts (Parrinder 1954:48; Herskovits 1962:294).

With the collapse of colonialism, modernization has come more and more into focus in the Third World. An awareness of activities around the globe, the wide gap between poverty and affluence that is so visible, the crime problem, nationalism, the variation of living standards, and many other factors have brought and kept the subject of modernization in focus. In the past twenty-five years modernization has been researched by historians, sociologists, anthropologists, philosophers, and psychologists. Let us take a good look at what is meant by modernization and gain a better understanding of the process that takes place.

ESSENTIAL CHARACTERISTICS OF MODERNIZATION

Everett Rogers has defined modernization as "the process by which individuals change from a traditional way of life to a more complex, technologically advanced, and rapidly changing style of life" (1969:14). I will use this definition of the term, recognizing that it implies cultural change in the direction of more complexity, a higher technology, and a faster speed of change than is normal within culture. Change is taking place in any given culture all the time; it is natural, and the people are comfortable with it and understand it. However, often the speed or duration of change in the modernization process leaves the people without an understanding of what is happening.

Modernization is not synonymous with *Westernization* or *Europeanization,* as is often perceived. David Kopf, a historian, notes that modernization is not a simple case of diffusion from one culture to another:

> In the first place, 19th century Europe was not so much the model for modernity as it was the setting for modernizing processes that were themselves transforming Western cultures.... The industrialization of culture patterns as diverse as those of Germany, Japan, and Russia was not only accomplished without benefit of British-style social and political institutions but was deliberately formulated in opposition to the British model. (1982:18)

We cannot assume that modernization is the same in two different countries. To understand modernization in any geographical area it is necessary to study the setting and the traditions.

Too often we see and judge others as "like us" if they speak English, use our technology, dress Western, work on our schedules, and so on. A deeper understanding of modernization will bring about a clearer understanding of people in other societies. Before relating spiritual-power concepts to culture change, we will examine some essential characteristics of modernization. These generalizations are largely based on Berger (1977); Berger, Berger, and Kellner (1973); Poggie and Lynch (1974); and Rogers (1969).

1. Modernization must be understood as a process. There is no such thing as "modern society" or "modern man" plain and simple; modernization is not a state of being. Rather we have a continuum of modernization. Within a society one finds a great variety of levels of modernization at a given point in time. Different segments of society modernize at different rates of speed. Often great differences exist between rural and urban, male and female, the elite and the masses, rich and poor, those formally educated and those without formal education.

2. The modernization process is multidimensional. This process cannot be measured by a single criterion. Too often technological production, which is quite measurable and obvious, is used alone to measure modernization. Literacy, rationalization, family solidarity, aspirations, political participation, bureaucracy, and meaningful lifestyle are other possible criteria.

3. The modernization process creates an impersonal idiom. This involves the dichotomization between public and private life. Paul Hiebert distinguishes between "multiplex" and "simplex" roles (1976:148–50). In multiplex relationships one meets the same person in many different social situations and so has a better chance of knowing the whole person. Modernization leads to simplex role relationships where one sees certain people only at work, others only at church, others only in the store, others only in the neighborhood. This causes adjustment and stress and a search for identity.

Berger, Berger, and Kellner refer to the "homeless mind" in their discussion of modernization and its effect on the consciousness:

> The reciprocity between individual and society, between subjective identity and objective identification through roles, now come to be experienced as a sort of struggle. Institutions cease to be the "home" of the self, instead they become oppressive realities that distort and estrange the self. Roles no longer actualize the self, but serve as a "veil of *maya*" hiding the self not only from others but from the individual's own consciousness. (1973:93)

When life becomes fragmented in role relationships, no one knows the whole person — we know only a part of a person according to what the particular role relationship is. It becomes difficult to find security in the people one knows.

Impersonalness is also found on the job, where only one's services are needed, not the whole person. Being paid in cash or with a check and on a time basis brings little true affirmation for the actual work done. The employer's concern and evaluation are only in terms of the quality and quantity of work that are being accomplished. In business an impersonal mediator is often used to solve problems and make things run smoothly.

4. Modernization brings the constant threat of meaninglessness due to never identifying the whole. As life becomes fragmented, it becomes difficult, if not impossible, to focus on the whole. If involved in production, one is likely doing just a part of the process. If one works as a laborer, the clock likely determines how much one has accomplished — not the finishing of the project. Private life often becomes regimented around activities requiring one to be away from home. One experiences the transformation of time with endless striving and restlessness.

5. Modernization often requires the formation of new roles and adjustment to old roles. This involves moving from ascribed roles to achieved roles. In the latter persons must prove themselves in a competitive market in order to have a job. Male/female roles often need to be adjusted when the husband must spend much more time away from home or when the

wife is holding a job away from home also. It often means moving from "self-employment" in farming or herding to becoming a part of a bureaucratic system. Leadership roles may shift from the elders to the wealthy or schooled. "Modernization legitimates new experts and simultaneously delegitimates old ones" (Berger, Berger, and Kellner 1973:146).

6. Bureaucracy is often present in the modernization process. A bureaucracy locates the individual in the system where he/she is expected to operate with regular procedures. One is assigned a sphere of life in the system and is held accountable only for that area. The rights and duties that must be followed are a part of the bureaucratic office. The person working for the bureaucratic agency and its clients also tends to become anonymous. A relatively educated middle class often emerges that derives its position from employment in the bureaucratic apparatus.

7. Technological production is a primary carrier of modernization. Workers are hired for their productive activity and become a part of a large organization with a few knowledgeable experts at the top. Some of the concomitants of technological production at the level of consciousness are: the segregation of work from private life, the separability of means and ends, anonymous social relations, a componential self (the self being experienced in a partial and segmented way), and the constant threat of meaninglessness due to never identifying the whole (Berger, Berger, and Kellner 1973:27–37).

8. Modernization helps develop a consciousness of a world beyond the limits of everyday social experiences. Formal education, military service, and mass communication cause one to begin comparing one's own situation to the world setting, to begin thinking new thoughts and dreaming new dreams. Individuals then become more private because not all in their society have experienced the same things, and they have sources for new information to which not everyone has access. In school students learn not only reading, writing, and arithmetic, but to think independently, to be more time-oriented, to be open to new ideas, to be more informed about the world, to be more individualistic. Mass media also present new ideas and allow the viewer or reader to experience more of the world. In the military the individual gets new status, new identity, new meaning in the group, and vision for the future.

MODERNIZATION IN RELATION TO TRADITIONAL SOCIETIES

When modernization comes to a society, certain persons welcome it and the new ideas, things, projects, and practices that come from outside. But there are some who choose their traditional ways and a slower pace of culture change. There is a danger for those who have chosen modernization and for those from outside the culture to give a valuation of superiority to those who "become modern" over those who "remain traditional." This puts up barriers that hinder communication between the two groups. In reality, modernization brings both constructive and destructive effects to society.

Traditional societies often are in close touch with the natural environment, whereas the modernization process tends to focus more on production, increased efficiency, and change. To illustrate, Margaret Mead explains how "the Indian" had a symbolic relationship to the environment:

> The Indian who, after he had eaten a fish, put the bones back in the creek and said, "Little brother, go back and be born again so I can eat you again" was symbolically talking about recycling. That is a perfect mythological, religious, poetic statement of recycling in which man recognizes that he is a part of nature and that his life depends upon recognizing that he is part of nature instead of standing apart from it. (1974:34)

Modernization, in extending human capacities to accomplish good for the society, has often caused wastefulness and loss of perspective on the environment.

In the more traditional settings there is cooperation and redistribution of wealth to meet everyone's needs. Face-to-face interaction in multiple roles, fine-tuned interpersonal relationships, the satisfaction of knowing who you are and where you belong in society — these are all a part of the person-orientation found in traditional societies. The whole person is in focus, and production is based on need with every part of the crop or animal being used in some way. Richard N. Adams points out that technological advancement has increased both the concentration of power and wealth and the gap between the highly developed and the less developed. Increased production of goods requires an increase in the production of waste: "The production of waste and the marginalization of societies are merely the physical and social aspects of the single process of development" (1974:38). The marginalized people are those excluded from participation in the controls of the system, those furthest removed from the centers of power. Exploitation of some people often takes place. Modernization must not be considered intrinsically superior to whatever was before and must be examined carefully.

Homer G. Barnett, an anthropologist who specialized in culture change, provides assistance in understanding the process of modernization. He based his model for change on the recombination of cultural elements. Culture change begins with individual change, which becomes part of the group norm as others adopt it. The worldview of the receptor is very important in this process. The innovator first identifies two things as equal or alike, or perhaps with the same function. He/she draws on that which is familiar in order to account for that which is new. Barnett emphasized that innovation is "a creation only in the sense that it is a new combination, never in the sense that it is something emerging from nothing" (1953:181). Thus "discovery" always builds on what is already there. Barnett's theory of culture change emphasizes conceptual relationships and their combination.

Modernization is often brought about by the process of acculturation, the cultural adjustment that takes place when two distinct cultures come into contact with each other. Sometimes the traditional society is forced to change when another society interferes actively and forcefully with it. Directed culture change often involves inhibiting the practice of preexisting cultural patterns. However, certain forms of behavior are the only elements of culture that can be forced on another society. Attitudes and values cannot be forced because the receptor society interprets according to its own value system. If there is inhibition of preexisting patterns, some of the needs of the society are left unsatisfied and hardship results. Ralph Linton writes:

> Under culture change which is both directed and enforced, the normal processes of retention of old elements until satisfactory substitutes have been found is inhibited.... This leaves certain of the group's needs unsatisfied, produces derangements in all sorts of social and economic relationships and results in profound discomfort for the individuals involved. (Linton 1940:9)

This has often been the case in colonialism, with enforced culture change causing frustration and difficulties. Under normal processes of culture change the old is retained until a satisfactory substitute has been found. In modernization changes may come too fast for this to happen.

In the postcolonial era, nations are desiring to find their identities apart from the power that ruled them. Tradition, rightly so, is seen as the framework for modernization. Joseph Gusfield explains how entwined tradition and modernization are and the need to look carefully at each situation:

> We cannot easily separate modernity and tradition from some specific tradition and some specific modernity, some version which functions ideologically as a directive. The modern comes to the traditional society as a particular culture within its own traditions. (1967:361)

Nationalism often entails balancing the modern and the traditional in a meaningful way. Choices are made as to language use, dress, music, celebration days, male/female dynamics, political structures, economic patterns, and subjects to be taught at school. Gusfield states:

The desire to be modern and the desire to preserve tradition operate as significant movements in the new nations and developing economies. It is our basic point here that these desires functioning as ideologies are not always in conflict; that the quest for modernity depends upon and often finds support in the ideological upsurge of traditionalism. (1967:358)

Modernization takes place by building on the traditional and at times consciously promoting selected traditional ways and values. For some societies, the answer to the mix of the traditional and modern ways is worked out by compartmentalization. Milton Singer (1966) writes of the Brahmans in India who have two separate spheres of living. At work the language is English and the dress is Western, with foreign-originated behaviors acceptable (even ignoring the caste rules). At home and in social relations the language, dress, and behavior change to traditional. For these Hindus both secularization and "Sanskritization" is taking place. The latter term refers to increased conformity to Hindu beliefs and practices. The adaptation that is taking place can be illustrated by a Hindu industrialist who in his reinterpretation of basic Hindu doctrine said that when he is going to be reborn he would prefer to be an industrialist again, except that instead of taking a B.S. in geology he would prefer to have a B.A. in economics (Singer 1966:61).

In summary, the modernization process is built on the traditions of a society, so each culture is distinctive in its blend of the two. In some cases the individual becomes bicultural and lives comfortably in two worlds. More often traditional values and practices continue on mixed with modern technology, formal education, new bureaucratic structures, and new job situations.

CONCEPTS OF SPIRITUAL POWER

What are the effects of the modernizing process on concepts of spiritual power? One effect is that although focus on the spiritual is lessened, the basic understanding of the spiritual makeup of the world continues. When a person begins depending on others for food, work, a place to live, and transportation, that person experiences a loss of control and security, creating tension and the need for assistance. Calling on spiritual powers brings relief and hope. Living in new territory often entails a new set of active spirits to be recognized and on which to call. When people are marginalized in society and no longer have control, control is sought in spiritual powers. Many of the adjustments brought about by modernization require more assistance from spiritual powers; these adjustments include adapting to, for instance, new roles, the fragmented life, a new societal structure, pressures to achieve for status purposes, and independent living away from the extended family.

In the West the emphasis on causality never fully banished involvement with the spiritual world, even long after the Reformation and the Enlightenment. This is shown in the belief in and practice of magic and witchcraft for a long period of time. Today the continuation of witchcraft and sorcery in the non-Western world indicates a worldview that assumes the activity of spiritual power.

Traditional beliefs and values have been observed to hang on when students are preparing for Western professions. Leaving their homeland for studying abroad often brings suffering because of the contrast of worldviews. T. Adeoye Lambo, a professor of psychiatry in Nigeria, discovered that most of those who had psychological breakdowns while studying in Great Britain were struggling with traditional values:

> In a study of a group of Nigerian students who broke down during their courses of university study in Great Britain in 1957, it was found that the symptoms of more than 90% of the patients offered clear-cut evidence of African traditional beliefs in bewitchment and machinations of the enemy. The students tended to regard their dream-lives as objective reality. The appearance of dead persons in dreams thus took on a quality of reality with deep psychological significance. (1964:445)

When there is stress, either emotional or otherwise, newly acquired social attitudes and ideologies are more susceptible to "damage," and the traditional beliefs and indigenous moral philosophy take over.

Another indication of continued belief in the spiritual is seen in how worldview interacts with technological change. In order to live in society as it is, not as it once was, people use their values and beliefs to integrate the new things of technology into life. In south India, for instance, there was a case of modernization in which a buffalo was sacrificed to a motorbike (Whitehead 1921:89). Animal sacrifices were used in this geographical area largely for propitiation. The animal was taken before the altar and decapitated, and blood was sprinkled on the object before which the sacrifice was offered. Traditionally when a well was sunk or a new tool or agricultural implement was used, all of which might be the means of causing death, an animal sacrifice was offered in appeasement to the evil spirit. In this case the motorbike, a sign of modernization, was given the traditional ritual and ceremony for safety.

Today we often find a conscious blending of the traditional and the modern. T. Adeoye Lambo reports that in his care for the mentally ill he collaborates with the traditional healers. Confession, dancing, and ritual are used powerfully in psychotherapy:

> Concepts of health within the framework of African cultures are far more social than biological. In the mind of the African, there is a more unitary concept of psychosomatic interrelationship, that is, an apparent reciprocity between mind and matter. Health is not an isolated phenomenon but part of the entire magico-religious fabric; it is more than the absence of disease. (1964:446)

Recognizing the spiritual beliefs and dealing with them bring about integration and help in the individual's adjustment in the modernization process.

A society's worldview is learned largely unconsciously in the enculturation process. Children are conditioned to interpret the reality around them according to the basic assumptions and values of the society. In the next chapter we will look more specifically at how change has affected the Navajo, Thai, and Kamwe worldview. In each a consciousness of spiritual presence and interaction is felt at a deep level. As new technology and ideas are adopted into a culture, the meaning and behavioral responses are processed through the worldview.

Chapter 10

Worldview Change in the Case Studies

With a clearer understanding of the process of modernization, its various relationships to traditional societies, and some various responses to modernization, we next look at the three case studies. The question to be dealt with is, How does the process of modernization influence worldview and the belief in spiritual powers? Here we must keep in mind the role of felt needs in the modernizing process.

THE NAVAJO AND SPIRITUAL POWERS IN MODERN TIMES

According to the Navajo worldview, spiritual experience provides the meaningful integration of society. The Navajos' sense of spiritual oneness with their surroundings brings a feeling of reverence for all forms of life. The Navajos in their consciousness of the spiritual dimension of life recognize their personal need for assistance from these powers in daily life — to be enriched, admonished, guided, and strengthened. Since it is the individual's responsibility to be open to these powers, there is a variety of ways to accomplish this.

Modernization has brought a choice of religious practices and beliefs to this very spiritually oriented people. The type of specific need, the availability of the family, the cost of the ritual, the time factor, and the credibility of the local leaders all affect which of three religions (Christianity, Peyotism, and traditional religion) a Navajo will choose at any given time. Only Christianity has an exclusivistic definition of membership, practice, and belief. Many Christian groups require that members do not participate in non-Christian religious rituals, but some do not make an issue of the exclusiveness. So it is not uncommon to find Navajos practicing all three religions for different situations in life.

In spite of the coming of Christianity and Peyotism to the reservation, traditional religion continues to be practiced. The "singer," often referred to as the medicine man, and the diviners are still active. For instance, a number of years ago ten singers participated in a ground blessing ceremony for the Navajo Culture and Heritage Center at Tes Bonito Park (*Navajo Times* 15, no. 40, 1974).

Since World War II, when many Navajo were in the service or working off the reservation in war industries, there has been a new interest in improving health care on the reservation. There is a combination of beliefs about the cause and cure of disease that differentiates between the white man's sickness and traditional sickness. Sometimes the diviners recommend white doctors, and sometimes they recommend a Peyote meeting in place of or along with a certain traditional curing ceremony. John Adair and Kert Deuschle write of the situation:

> The doctor could now have confidence that the patient would return for his treatment in the hospital if he was allowed to go home for a Sing. By the same token the medicine man was confident that his patient whose pneumonia did not respond to his treatment would come back to him for completion of the ritual. (1970:30)

Often a sing is performed before or after a regular hospital visit to ensure that harmony is restored. If the patient fails to respond to curing ceremonies and modern medicine, witchcraft is suspected. A more powerful ceremony is then required to deal with such evil powers.

Today a growing number of mental health professionals are working in cooperation with the traditional therapists (the singers) (Jilek and Jilek-Aall 1981:20). Because of Navajo worldview it is necessary for the traditional and the modern to be used together in medical treatment.

Christianity was first presented to the Navajos without considering their worldview assumptions and values. In fact, it was introduced as part of helping the federal government "civilize" them. The focus on harmony, the felt need for curing ceremonies as required by daily events, the existence of evil spirit powers, and the existing social structure were all overlooked (Reichard 1944). The Navajos' position has been described in these terms:

> Navajos, like other animists, are not about to give up their gods for some intellectual, theoretical religion. They are convinced of the reality of spiritual forces and can point to many demonstrations of their existence. They want a god who is able to meet their needs.... The majority of Navajo ceremonies are for the purpose of healing and the

people equate healing with supernatural activity. (Dolaghan and Scates 1978:66–67)

Only in the last three decades has Christianity been attractive to many Navajo adults. My interviewing showed that conversion for many adults in the church today has often come at a time of family crisis or a time of physical healing through Christian prayer, through a vision, or through some direct answer to a need for spiritual power.

Where the church has grown, Navajo culture has been taken seriously. Many missions have adjusted to the Navajo time for interacting with spiritual power by having all or most of their worship services after dark. Local leadership in the church has been or is being turned over to Navajos. Christian meetings are expanding beyond the "neutral" territory of the mission compound to the home area in the form of tent meetings. Food is served after the several-hour night meeting, and this is more like the Navajo way. The practice of having Christian tent meetings on family property has made it easy and natural for non-Christian relatives to attend.

Indigenous leaders recognize the spiritual need for healing and protection, and they readily speak to those issues. The body of Christians is often mobilized for specific action when a need arises in the daily life of a particular Christian. As I participated with a Christian church group I observed the creative way in which help was given when needed. For instance, at one point a disaster fell on a Navajo pastor's family. After four days of gathering assistance from family and church, there was a good turn of events. The church family then gathered to rejoice and to pray for God's protection from evil powers in the future. A Christian relative announced to the group who had gathered that he had had a vision the night before in which Jesus as the Rock was prominent. So he instructed the pastor to go out and get five rocks to be prayed over. After the prayer anointing the family and the rocks, he instructed the pastor to place one rock in the house to remind him of Jesus as the Rock and then to go out the next morning before sunup and bury one rock to the north, one to the south, one to the east, and one to the west in order to protect the family from evil powers. The importance of the four directions in Navajo thinking and the credibility given to visions were obvious here.

The Peyote religion uses forms from both traditional religion and Christianity. It does not see the ways of the Navajo as inferior, and there is a feeling of pride and identity as Navajos are fully in charge of the meetings. The practices of Peyotism fit very well with the worldview concepts of the Navajo. Illness is seen as a product of spiritual forces, and cure then must be through dealing with the spiritual. Peyotism recognizes how important relationship with spiritual power is in daily well-being. It offers a means of power to meet felt needs as well as to give new meaning to life.

It supplies inner peace and harmony through interaction with spirit powers, confession time, and time for reflection. It provides both new power for old purposes (for example, witchcraft, dealing with ghosts, and physical healing) and new power for the new sources of danger (for example, alcohol, family breakdown, uncontrollable temper). It also supplies a standard of morality including abstinence from alcohol, faithfulness to the family, control of temper, and sexual restraint. With the scattering of the family and a breakdown in the social control, this is very useful.

In the early days the Peyotists saw their religion as an Indian version of Christianity, but today they see themselves as traditionalists and supporters of Navajo religion (Aberle 1982:xlv). Peyotists could see their religion as an Indian version of Christianity because, like Christianity, their religion addressed a new deity; the singer (an aspect of the traditional religion) was by-passed, and, as in Christianity, the individual could now have direct contact with spiritual power; the leader was a self-appointed priest; and the language in prayer reflected Christian terms: Our Father, God, Jesus, Mary, and the heavenly angels. Peyotism was new to the Navajo, like Christianity, and did not use the rigidly fixed formula in prayers as was used in traditional religion.

Today, when there is great pride in being Navajo, Peyotists see themselves as traditionalists. The setting, the arrangement of people, the observance of the power of the four directions, the performance of the four parts to the ritual with four songs in each group, the timing and place of the ceremony, the need for the ceremony — all are related to traditional religious beliefs and assumptions.

The modern world presents dangers still, and some Navajos use amulets for safety and protection. An interviewee explained how her husband, who died in a car accident, had been wearing amulets with Peyote and corn pollen for protection. She said that if there was power there he would not have died. She left Peyotism after that experience. For many Navajos lightning, snakes, and witchcraft all continue to represent evil power.

For the Navajo, one's well-being in the modern world is linked to harmony and balance between all of life. Carl Gorman, a Navajo writer for the *Navajo Times,* writes that all illness is being out of harmony with nature; that is, it involves transgression against one's body in excesses of various kinds; failure to keep one's thoughts pure and harmonious; and/or lack of knowledge, will, or power to keep the evil thoughts of others from harming one (*Navajo Times* 15, no. 40, 1974). It is necessary for there to be a balance between the individual and his/her total physical environment and between the spirit power and human beings.

The Navajo worldview is person-oriented. How the person fits in society, the relationship and obligation to clan members, who you can trust and who you need to fear, these are all carefully spelled out in a face-to-face society. James F. Downs has explained the transition to modernization and the difficulties it has brought:

> The basic problem is a transition from a system in which persons trusted individuals rather than institutions to one which is, in effect, quite the opposite. In the past, the individual knew which persons he could trust because of their ritual knowledge, their position in his kinship system, or their proven ability in face-to-face situations with which he had personal experience. Today he is asked to depend on such vague concepts as the law, justice, the tribal government, or the federal constitution. (1972:128)

When a Navajo male leaves the reservation for work, he usually finds a very impersonal world. His family usually stays on the reservation, so he is away from his family and clan involvement. He experiences a loss of social status in moving from the relative self-determination that he had. In the new environment he is important to no one and is usually viewed as lower class. His job occupies only a specific number of hours per day, so he has free time. Having his wages paid weekly is often a new experience. Many spiritual powers that are important to him are related to and often depend upon his former surroundings, so unknown powers cause him tension. When the family/clan is needed for ceremonies to restore harmony, he is away from home. In my interviewing I was made aware of the tremendous difficulty these men have in adjusting. Drinking, fighting, and carousing often resulted due to the stresses of living and trying to exist in a foreign world. Many told of the attempts they made to get their lives straightened out through Peyote ceremonies or traditional religious ceremonies. Two of my interviewees told of a clear vision from God at that time that gave them hope and caused them to turn to Christianity for direction for living.

During World War II, thirty-six thousand Navajos entered the armed forces and were transported to all parts of the world. Evon Vogt researched the changing values of Navajo veterans who had returned to Navajo society (1951). The aspects of the Navajo system that were more resistant to change included the belief in and fear of ghosts and witches, divination as practiced by the Navajo hand-tremblers, the concept of the universe being full of dangers, present-orientation, event-orientation, and the quest for harmony (Vogt 1951:115, 134). Almost all of these worldview concepts relate to their assumptions about spiritual power. However, the veterans had changed to accept white medicine for most illnesses, thus losing the belief in the efficacy of the curing chants for such cases.

THE THAI AND SPIRITUAL POWER IN MODERN TIMES

How has modernization affected Thai worldview and belief in spiritual power? Charles Keyes writes:

No matter what the degree of modernization, traditional ideas, nonetheless, still continue to be widely held. Moreover, few villagers who have adopted new ideas reject the fundamental concepts of the traditional system. Ideas concerning merit and demerit involved in the conception of Karma... continue to provide the grounding for the cultural meanings that villagers throughout the region use in adapting to the world as they experience it. (1977:125–26)

Buddhist ideology motivates those with wealth to use some of it for merit making. They can enjoy the comforts that wealth obtains because it is indicative of previous good karma. Only for those who become monks is poverty seen as a virtue. Thai culture may still be summed up in one word — religion, with the beliefs and practices of Buddhism, Brahmanism, and animism.

Spirit houses, located on hotel property, university property, and outside homes and places of business, affirm the activity of spirits. The importance of spiritual assistance is obvious during exam time at the university when the spirit house is crowded with flowers and gifts. A large spirit house in Bangkok is busy day and night. Flower sellers are there, and the flowers placed on the shrine have to be cleared away two or more times a day. Dancers can be hired to dance in front of the shrine. People travel to this powerful spirit house for spirit power to win the lottery, to become pregnant, to solve marital problems, and to deal with business reversals and other personal difficulties (Hill 1985).

Spirit possession, done in order to serve the needs of the Thai, is on the increase as more people move to the city. In the urban setting, with unfamiliar spirits around and with the family unit more scattered, new problems arise that need spiritual assistance for solution. An interviewee informed me how a person who had had his motorcycle stolen went to a well-known medium to get help from a spirit for his problem (Taeng 1985). The medium told him that it had been stolen and painted and where he could find it. He went to the police, and together they went to that place and recovered the motorcycle.

As new jobs are created by urbanization, psychological pressures and personal conflict increase also. Changes in the structure of society and new expectations in the work environment bring the need for outside power in order to meet tensions:

> Persons who have migrated to the cities to fill the new roles in the mid-
> dle ranges of governmental and private bureaucracies seem to have lost
> their village or kinship connections without having as yet developed
> an urban or occupational identity. To express their personal conflicts
> they turn to traditional means, black magic, and to relieve their anxi-
> ety they take part in spirits (at *lak muang* temples) in Thailand. (Evers
> 1973:113)

Again change causes the Thai to reach out for spiritual power with new
interest in religion and magic.

Modernization has made Western medicine available, so today when illness strikes, the person/family must make a choice as to the cause. Some go
to a medium or call in a spirit doctor. Others go to the clinic or hospital.
Some whom I interviewed said they first went to the hospital, but when they
were not helped there, they went to a medium or a spirit doctor. Two of these
received immediate healing when they followed the instructions of the local
practitioner (Saowkaweow 1985; Tat 1985).

In the modern world traditional ceremonies have broad use. The house-
blessing ceremony, which is a traditional ceremony, is still performed on a
finished house before anyone can enter it. The monks, after encircling the
house with a holy white cord and reciting blessings, enter the house and chant
for some time. Holy water is sprinkled around the house to prevent bad luck
and evil spirits from entering. An interviewee reported that sometimes when
one buys a car in the city, a ceremony is held and string is tied around the
car to keep those who will use it safe (Subinraht 1985). A spirit doctor who
mediates with the spirit world would be in charge, and often the ancestor
spirits would be called on at this time.

In the past there has been pressure for all males to serve as novices or
monks sometime in their lives. However, today such service is not tied so
closely with becoming an adult. A special title of respect and deference is
used for monks, and they are then qualified to be the religious leaders of the
community. There is no stigma whatsoever in leaving the monkhood. Some
men are only a monk for the three months of Buddhist Lent, others for a few
years, and a few remain monks all of their lives.

Modernization has changed the role of the monk some as most of the formal education of children is no longer in temple schools, but separate from
the monastery. Other functions the monks used to perform that have been
taken over by government agencies are practicing traditional medicine and
practicing traditional techniques in architecture, well digging, and sculpture
(Suksamran 1977:19). Monks, however, are the mediators of Buddha-power
and are very active today. They have renounced the world but are very thoroughly involved in the society around them. As discussed earlier, they infuse

spiritual power into water, Buddha images, tattooing, amulets, and other charms. By chanting powerful mantras they can resist evil powers. They know the auspicious times of power and are called on to set the date/time for a marriage, funeral, or the opening of a new business. Monks give blessings as requested on many special occasions, for example, birthdays, times of sickness, and marriage. They are *always* called for the ceremonies at the time of death; they transfer merit to the person who has died as well as to all who have come to listen. In modern times, monks give advice, cooperate, and participate in communal activities of development, for example the construction of a village well, building a bridge or small dam, repairing a school.

Today because of modern jobs, improved transportation, and education people are traveling away from their home area to places where they are unfamiliar with the spirit world around them. Since Thai worldview recognizes the reality of active spirits who can help or harm human beings, the unpredictability of the environment brings about an increase in the use of amulets for protection. Persons of any age, both male and female, carry them for protection.

Christianity, which has had a presence in Thailand for over one hundred years, has been accepted by only .06 percent of the Thai population, according to the 1970 census (Barrett 1982:664). A big problem has been that Christianity has often been seen as a religious system that tries to replace Buddhism, and Thai identity is tied up in Buddhism. Philip Hughes notes that the early Thai Christians were social outcasts, slaves, socially ostracized people, and those driven to the missionary by epidemics and famine (1982:93–95). In spite of the small number of converts, the missionaries have been involved in the modernization process:

> They brought important forms of human liberation in their introduction of women's education, vaccines, educational techniques, hospitals, and new technologies. People accused of demon possession, people in poverty, lepers...they found a hope in missionary Christianity they could not find in society. (Swanson 1984:iv)

However, the church that was established was foreign and had very little to do with Thai culture.

THE KAMWE AND SPIRITUAL POWER IN MODERN TIMES

Modernization for the Kamwe began with the construction of roads, which brought motor transport into the area, making it possible for them to obtain goods from the outside and export peanuts to the outside world.

Primary schools were established, but when a child wanted to continue on in secondary school, it was often necessary to go outside the Kamwe area.

Gradually since the middle of the twentieth century, more and more Kamwe have gone to the city for work and for further education. At first it was on an individual basis, but now many Kamwe families are city dwellers:

> A strong sense of mutual obligations sustains ties of kinship as the dominant concern of everyday life. Every member of the family group has status, rights and obligations, and enjoys the sense of security which comes from these. He is protected against unemployment, old age, the cost of sickness, and can appeal to it in any difficulty. In return, he will be expected to support others, to contribute to family celebrations, to attend meetings, and reciprocate visits. (Marris 1962:39)

When one moves to the city there is usually some extended family to help one get established. When things do not go well in the city or when one is ready to retire, there is a place available in the home area. This sense of belonging to the family as a whole gives the Kamwe a sense of emotional security that is helpful during the modernization process. On a recent visit to Nigeria, I saw several large, Western-style homes built in the rural small towns by retired government workers or retired educators who had returned to their home area after retirement.

Modernization has weakened the authority structure of the family. As individual family members have scattered for schooling or work or have become Christian, the traditional ceremony held in the household (*malya*) and performed by the elder of the house for the well-being of the members of the house has ceased to be practiced in many areas of Kamweland. When children go away from the home area for school or work, they often meet and marry someone their family does not even know. In the past the parents carefully checked the entire family of the potential bride or groom before making final arrangements for the marriage. Now young people often make the choice of a mate, and parents cannot force them to marry anyone else.

Another sign of the weakening of family (and ancestor) control is the increase in sexual immorality. In the past the girls were "protected" by the living arrangement at home and early arranged marriages. Now the age for girls to marry is older, and they are at boarding schools and away from home. The result is a rise in unwanted pregnancies, abortions, and births before marriage (Taru 1990). Both the local herbalist's prescription and modern medicine from the chemist are used for abortions. Prostitution even in towns and villages is on the rise also.

Today there are special areas where spirits are very active, making it dangerous to pass there. One of these places is a bridge near a town where many accidents have occurred. People fight more and have accidents in these spirit-infested places (Taru 1990).

The great numbers of amulets in use today by both Christians and non-Christians affirm the belief in active spiritual powers. Children often wear amulets for protection from the evil spirits. Adults also use amulets to gain spiritual power and protection from witchcraft, sorcery, and curses.

Western medicine has been widely accepted in many Kamwe areas for the quick results it brings, especially for sudden illnesses. However, for chronic long diseases and for cases where Western medicine is ineffective, the herbal doctor or spirit doctor is contacted for treatment.

In an interview a medicine woman, who is a well-known practitioner in a wide area, explained that she deals with physical ailments including barrenness (Bazza 1990). She does not deal with spirits because of the danger to her as a woman and to her twelve children. She sends people to the male spirit doctor nearby when it is necessary. She learned herbal treatment from her mother and grandmother, who were practitioners. The interviewee became a baptized Christian in 1979 and goes to church regularly, refusing to practice medicine on Sundays. She explained that prayer and the power of God give the medicine more potency. She has combined a relationship with God with her practice of traditional medicine.

The church has incorporated meaningful symbols from the culture: guinea corn instead of bread for Communion, local tunes for church songs, the drum as accompaniment in worship, a special Christian ceremony for planting guinea corn, and the local dance-style for special Christian celebrations. Ninety percent of the Christian marriages follow the traditional wedding ritual with prayers to God through Christ added at important times (the other 10 percent have Western weddings, which are very expensive) (Guli 1990).

According to the response of many older people, the Christian funeral has not met felt needs, and some old men and women leave the church in order to have a traditional burial. The new funeral form buries the person the same day, has a Western-type service, and buries the person in a place away from the family burial grounds. The traditional ceremony lasts several days, so all the relatives can get there, and involves traditional music and dancing, eating food together, audible crying, and honoring the person who has died. There is also drinking and sexual immorality. As the family and community celebrate together, grief is expressed and the adjustment to life without the person begins. The spirit is ushered with honor into the place of the ancestors.

I have illustrated the effect of modernization on the spiritual-power beliefs in the worldviews of three different societies. The response of each society to modernization is distinct, and the previous basic assumptions and values are a part of the process. Felt needs and worldview definitely influence and shape the new behavior, technology, job situations, structures, and meanings in life.

PART IV

STRATEGY

Chapter 11

Missiological Application

We have examined the human need for spiritual power as seen in three different societies. Study of the Bible's depiction of God's power used on behalf of his people and to overcome other spiritual powers shows that the God of Christianity is powerful. For societies that are spiritual-power-oriented, needing spiritual power for everyday activities, it is necessary to consider making some adjustments to Christianity. These will involve the way the gospel is introduced, the biblical definition of the spirit world, the programming of Christian activity, the use of Scripture for daily living, and an emphasis on the power of Christ within the believer.

This chapter is divided into four sections in order to focus on the various aspects of application. The first section deals with using the receptor's understanding of the spirit realm for the initial communicating of the gospel to non-Christians. The second section deals with using this understanding to guide in individual Christian growth. The third section deals with shaping the church to meet the felt needs for spiritual power held by the believers. The fourth section deals with the relevance of spiritual beliefs in the non-Christian worldview to the contextualization of Christianity.

INITIAL COMMUNICATION OF THE GOSPEL

In communication theory the role of the receptor is paramount to effective communication (C. Kraft 1991a:67–80). The receptors decide if the communicator and/or message are credible, if the message is relevant to their values, if the message meets any of their felt needs and therefore should be considered, and how much risk is involved in listening. In fact, the actual meaning of the message is reconstructed in the minds of the receptors according to their worldview, experiences, and cultural conditioning.

The following are some specific suggestions for the initial communication of the gospel. They are based on the three case studies presented.

1. For the Navajos, to whom nature is very sacred, the gospel message can be made more credible if there is emphasis on passages from the Word that speak of God's creation and care for all he has created, of harmony between all he created, and of human responsibility to keep that harmony (for example, Psalms 104; Genesis 1 and 2). Many passages in the Old Testament speak of the physical environment and of how God works and speaks through it. God demonstrates his power to keep nature in balance. Recognition of God's place in nature could well be a part of regular corporate worship.

2. In order to meet the felt need of dealing with evil spiritual power (in all three societies studied), God must be presented as one who is knowledgeable and has power over evil. For the Thai and the Kamwe much effort is placed on warding off evil spirits, and in all three societies when something goes wrong it is often perceived to be the action of evil spirit power. The cross-cultural communicator must recognize the activity that takes place between the spirit world and humans (see Eph. 6:12) and be ready to let God be victorious. For example, when a non-Christian child is ill (whether the perceived cause is offending a tree spirit or germs), the one bringing the message of Christ needs to be ready to pray audibly for healing from God to claim the power and authority God gives us (Luke 9:1). When treatment is given at a Christian, Western-style clinic or hospital, audible prayer needs to be a part of the treatment of each patient — reminding him/her of God's power in the healing and his power over the spirit world.

3. If the worldview does not focus on and prepare for an afterlife (the Navajo worldview being an example), eternal life in Christ will not attract the attention of the non-Christian. Without ignoring the fact of eternal life it would be much better to first focus on the felt needs of the present that are addressed also in the Scripture, such as family problems including troubled interpersonal relationships, barrenness, how to respond to witchcraft, preservation of the group when scattered geographically, and drunkenness. The focus needs to be on what Christ will do for today.

4. As already mentioned, according to Thai worldview the auspicious numbers are the odd ones. An uneven number of monks is required for rituals (except the death ritual), and special occasions are usually given on odd-numbered dates. Missionaries would be more acceptable if they used auspicious numbers in presenting the gospel. It is good to keep the receptor as comfortable and open as possible for the message. This might entail designing "five spiritual laws" or "nine spiritual laws" to replace the much-used "four spiritual laws."

5. The time of day, grouping of people, and place for assembling should be arranged considering the worldview of the receptor. For example, the Navajos traditionally have religious activity seeking spiritual interaction and power at night, with clan members, and on family property. The church ser-

vice in the morning, for "everyone," and on mission property is not very attractive. In recent decades the Christian message has been presented much more attractively at tent meetings, after dark, and in someone's yard. Non-Christian relatives often come and are open to hear about Christ and his relevance to them.

6. It is important to work with the group and group leaders in a society where the individual's identity is the group (such as the Kamwe). Working with the natural grouping is more apt to bring acceptable and long-lasting change. For the Kamwe the extended family is a spiritual group bound together through ancestor spirits. According to tradition the family needs to be united for religious ceremonies. The initial presentation of the gospel to the Kamwe was very low-key, as several older Kamwe men who had found Christ at the mission leprosarium and the mission eye hospital returned home (C. Kraft 1976). As they spoke informally with family elders and others in the family group there was time to discuss faith in Christ, to ponder the possibilities for change, weighing the ramifications, and to attempt to make their own decisions. It was only after several years that the church was formally established. This approach was comfortable, fitting into the Kamwe worldview, but would have been difficult for a missionary to carry out because of the limitations of a Western worldview with so much emphasis on dealing with the individual alone.

INDIVIDUAL SPIRITUAL GROWTH

When there is a positive response to Christ, the work of the Christian leader has only begun. Conversion involves giving allegiance to Christ, and that allegiance needs to be reaffirmed each day. Often in the past, conversion to Christ included conforming to the culture of the carrier of the message. When this happened, there were often large areas of living that were neglected. For example, the Kamwe, being an agricultural people, needed spiritual power to ensure a good crop. If the missionary is not aware of this and if a Western interpretation of the Bible is practiced, old forms of ritual may be rejected even though they are precisely the ones that meet this felt need.

When a person responds to God, there is direct interaction with God, and this means that all of life should be affected by the experience. God has provided the Bible as a guidebook for learning about himself and his standards for living so that the convert will be able to represent him in the world. Throughout Scripture the importance of being obedient to God is emphasized. God accepts those who respond to his invitation as they are, and then he gently and patiently helps them to be more like himself.

The worldview of the convert, then, is important because that is God's starting point. People interpret new truth from their own viewpoints, looking through their own worldview lenses. It will require considerable time to bring the basic assumptions and values in line with what the Bible says. (Note how difficult it is to have a biblical view of wealth in America even today.)* Here I want to suggest some specific ways to encourage worldview change for the converts in order to keep from promoting cultural conversion instead of Christian conversion (C. Kraft 1963). The focus will be on the spiritual beliefs and values of the three societies presented in the case studies.

1. There needs to be instruction on the greatness of the power of God and the existence of the powers of evil. Passages to be studied and learned would include 1 John 4:4; 5:4–5, 19. God at work in the Old Testament reveals his power over other gods and spirits (for example, 1 Samuel 5; 1 Kings 18; Isa. 44:6–20).

2. For both the Thai and the Kamwe much energy is exerted to ward off and placate the spirit beings. The new believer needs to learn to employ the power of God to overcome (not simply placate) those spirits. Passages that speak of God's protection should be studied, memorized, and used (for example, Ps. 27:1–6; 28:7; Luke 10:19–20; 1 Pet. 4:11; and Col. 1:9–14).

3. Instruction on the power of God available to the Christian is essential. God gives the Christian power over evil spirits (Luke 9:1; 10:19). Christ in each Christian in the form of the Holy Spirit is the source of power for doing God's work (Rom. 15:13–17). Wayne Dye points out how the power God gives is to serve his purposes:

> 1. God provides power to be the right sort of spiritual person, to be morally strong and to react as a Christian should to the trials of life. (Col. 1:10–11; Phil. 4:3; 1 Cor. 10:13; Eph. 6:10–12; Luke 22:32; Acts 16:5)
>
> 2. The second biblical purpose of spiritual power is to be able to do God's work more effectively. This means to speak prophetically and also to see healing and other miracles in answer to prayer and to serve other believers in practical ways. (Mic. 3:8; 2 Cor. 13:4; Eph. 3:7; 2 Cor. 12:12) (1982:43–45)

God's power is given not just for protection but for enabling his people to do his work. Those who convert to Christ must know that the Holy Spirit within them empowers them for living and confronting the spiritual powers that exist around them.

---

*Jesus recognized the problems that wealth brings (Matt. 6:19–21, 24; 19:14–26). For Christians wealth should be used to meet immediate needs and shared with others (Luke 6:30; 2 Cor. 9:11; 1 Tim. 6:9–11).

4. To help the convert relate effectively with his/her family and group, teachings from Scripture should be used (for example, Matt. 19:19; 1 Cor. 7:3; Eph. 5:23–25; John 13:34–35). The new believer needs to be taught to seek God's guidance in how much he/she should be involved in non-Christian ritual expected of members of the extended family. It is important to weigh what the Christian's actions communicate about God in each situation (James 1:5; Ps. 143:8–10).

5. When people sense a spiritual richness while alone with nature (as the Navajo traditionally have), the new believer in Christ should be encouraged to go out alone and meditate, using the Scriptures for obtaining God's guidance (for example, Psalms 25 and 119). My experience has been that outside activity planned by the churches usually involves games and activity, not silent meditation. To be sure that Christ is in focus, and not the pre-Christian powers, occasional sessions could be planned to share what God has been teaching. Time for listening to God is often left out when working from a Western worldview.

SHAPING THE CHURCH TO MEET FELT NEEDS

The local church has direct responsibility for its members. Cultural voids often emerge if felt needs for spiritual power are not reckoned with and met in the structure and practices of the church. These produce tension and, if not dealt with, often lead to syncretism.* If there is a cultural practice that needs to be rejected when one accepts Christ, the church needs to deal with two questions: What were its functions in society? and What kind of Christian substitutes could take its place? Following Christ is a way of life, and the Bible gives good practical guidance. Individual spiritual needs should be dealt with through the church. Since areas of life in which a person feels the need for spiritual assistance still exist after conversion, the church must seriously deal with how to meet these needs.

Functional substitutes — rituals or activities that fulfill the same function and satisfy the same needs — may be needed. Alan Tippett notes that the innovator of a substitute must be an insider if the substitute is to become permanent. Often functional substitutes fail because they are tried long after the church is established and the congregation holds partly Western and only slightly indigenous values (Tippett 1987:185). When the church leadership senses that members of the church are struggling with unmet needs, they should consider a functional substitute:

---

*Syncretism is a mix of beliefs from two different religions, with the result that the religion practiced is separate from either. Luzbetak in his excellent discussion of the subject defines syncretism as "any theologically untenable amalgam" (1988:360).

> The concept of functional substitute permits amazing diversity in ap-
> plication. A functional substitute may be a form, a ritual, a symbol,
> a role, an idea, a craft, an occupation, an artifact, an economic pat-
> tern, or it may even be the Christian religion itself under certain ideal
> circumstances. (Tippett 1987:186)

Sometimes practices that were prohibited by the first Christian missionaries
are years later revised with Christian meaning by the local pastors in order
to meet felt needs. First-generation converts are often most harsh in rejecting
old customs having to do with power because they associate those customs
with their old pre-Christian ways. The second and third generations no longer
see those customs as sacred, but only as cultural symbols.

Again I will present from the three case studies some suggestions for con-
sideration based on worldview conditioning and the need for spiritual power.

1. Rituals for the rites of passage often involve seeking spiritual assistance for transition from one stage of life to another. For the Thai with their
belief in the *khwan* spirit, which is likely to leave at transition time, there
may be an uncomfortableness among new believers that could be solved
through Christian ritual. It is right to look to Christ for all problems. It is best
if indigenous forms are used and Christian meaning is given to them. Care
must be taken to bring in as few foreign forms as possible, lest Christianity
be seen simply as a foreign religion.

2. The tendency in the West is to have most of the church activities sched-
uled in advance, that is, regular worship, outreach, and business meetings.
Having observed in the case studies the way non-Christian groups operate, I
see the need for the church to be flexible and open to responding to felt needs
for spiritual power as they arise. The church should be on call for emergen-
cies, such as when lightning strikes a Christian home in Navajoland, when a
person is going away and needs special protection and blessing in Thailand,
when a problem arises that needs spiritual assistance for solution among the
Kamwe. If the church shows interest, plans rituals with the people in focus, and/or makes a group of believers available, the Christian will be less
likely to seek divine guidance and protection elsewhere. God is interested
in the whole person. Often the structure of the church blocks the possibility
of meeting the needs for spiritual power. If the church structure is not flexible enough to allow groups to gather for ritual practices whenever necessary,
then the Christian will often return to using non-Christian ceremonies.

3. The place and the arrangement of people for the Christian ritual are
influenced by the worldview of the people. To the Navajo the home is the
right place for ritual for personal needs, with a circle around those in charge.
Both Peyote meetings and traditional curing ceremonies take place on the
homestead. By meeting emergency situations there the church can expose

non-Christian relatives to what God is doing. A Navajo family told me how their house had been struck by lightning. According to tradition that is a very serious evil attack, requiring one to abandon the house and build a new one (Ranger 1986). Since they were Christian, they called their pastor, who came to the home with a church group. They called on God to use his power over the evil spirits, to protect the family, and to purify and bless the house. The family moved back into the house, and the neighbors and non-Christian relatives were amazed — they had seen the power of God at work. The church needs to be available to move with God's power to meet the spiritual needs of the members.

Worldview affects the position and interaction of male and female in the church also. Historically Christianity as established by the West has had few women in church leadership. However, women's organizations or women's Bible studies within the framework of the church have been very popular in many parts of the world. In Nigeria, the Kamwe women — who, according to custom, leave their birth families to live near their husbands' families — have benefited greatly from women's organizations. They have bonded together with many similar felt needs. Women's choirs, outreach activities, and projects have been very beneficial to the growth of the church.

In reference to the mission churches in Calabar, Nigeria, Rosalind Hackett records how women have taken the initiative to set up prayer and discussion groups in their homes:

> Alternatively the women's organizations within the churches provide a legitimate context in which women may come together not just for religious but also for social, economic and cultural purposes. It seems that women obtain more religious satisfaction from these organizations, where they are able to act independently according to their own needs, and be heard as a collective voice, than from the official, male-dominated forms of worship. (1985:259)

In parts of the world where women operate in a separate sphere from men the spiritual needs of each sex should be examined and then dealt with.

African independent churches, which were started in reaction to mission churches, allow women a great deal of independence in religious activities. Some of these churches have been founded by women. The church membership is fairly evenly balanced between men and women, but older women especially may command the respect of the whole church. Divine revelation is given to both young and old women, and the men respect this. The emphasis on healing attracts women especially because of their felt needs:

> Given the pressures on women to perpetuate the lineage and the problems surrounding childbirth and rearing healthy children in a developing country whose medical facilities are still far from adequate, it is not surprising that women turn to these churches for total or supplementary support. We also should not ignore the supernatural beliefs or fears which surround conception and childbirth and which the independent churches treat as existential realities. (Hackett 1985:263)

These churches are meeting women where they are in their needs and worldview. In a society where men do not normally take orders from women, the power of the Holy Spirit working in and through women causes men to listen and respond. Hackett also notes that the independent churches provide opportunity and an acceptable place in society for women who have become "displaced persons" (through childlessness, divorce, or accusations of witchcraft) (1985:265).

4. In areas where the belief in evil spirits and their daily activity with human beings exists, the church needs to teach about God's power. One Christian I interviewed in Thailand explained his belief that at baptism Christians are given the power of Christ so that the demons do not have power over them (Songkham 1985). For the Thai, Christian ceremonies for baptism, for house dedication before moving in, for safety in a new car, for safety on a journey — all need to focus on God's power over the evil spirits and his protecting hand. Since ritual plays a very important part in enculturation, the church can be strengthened as group needs are met and the solidarity of the group is affirmed.

5. Biblical teachings — from both the Old and New Testaments — about power encounters and about the way God works with his people regarding his power should be kept in focus. Tippett emphasizes the fact that Scripture demands that the people of God be willing to be involved in power encounters:

> The works of the devil have to be *destroyed*. Sinful man is bound. Christ came to *unloose* him....I have given you...power-with-authority...over the power of the enemy....If the Christian takes up his place in the world, he is involved as a soldier of Christ both defensively and offensively. (1973:89–90)

Christians are told to be on the watch and ready to defeat the powers in faith and loyalty to God (1 Pet. 5:8). Even though Christ unmasked and disarmed the powers at the cross and hence the victory is certain (Col. 2:13–15), yet the battle continues (Eph. 6:12; 1 Cor. 15:24).

6. In all three of the societies studied, the individual is very closely tied to the group. The church should recognize that the individual never stands alone but has specific responsibility to his/her family. There may be times when the pastor on invitation of a church member could attend a traditional family celebration and give suitable prayers to God for the occasion, as well as for the health and well-being of all members. At any rate, the pastor should encourage Christians to be responsible in the eyes of their families — to arrange marriages for brothers and/or sisters if the father has died and the responsibility has been delegated to the Christian, to provide a goat when it is expected for a family celebration, to share income with parents, brothers, or others when necessary. Too often these activities have been evaluated in terms of a foreign worldview, and the importance and expectations of the group have been overlooked. If the Christian is not a responsible family member, the message of Christ that is heard is that God does not care about non-Christians, does not care about the family's welfare, and is out to destroy the family unity. It would be better to try to help the family see that a new dimension has been added and that God is on their side.

7. The church can also help affirm the importance of the group by developing the notion of the family of God. Initiation into the group should reflect the local culture by including training for group membership and signifying a new position in life with new responsibilities. The West has much to learn from other parts of the world about the meaning of being members in "the family of God." Based on this notion, a Christian might well share financial responsibility, help another member get started in business, take into his/her own home a Christian in need, or fund university or Bible-school training for a qualified person.

I observed on the Navajo reservation, when doing research, one way the group operates in the family of God. An elder in the church felt God wanted him to "admonish" the Navajo pastor. He *and his family,* including his married son and his son's wife, drove many miles to the pastor's home to discuss the matter. (In churches in the West this would most likely be handled between individuals.)

8. It could very well be that the group as perceived in terms of the local worldview would identify with the corporate body and corporate sin in the Old Testament. If so, the church would need to develop means to handle this concept. For corporate sin the guilt is shared by the entire group. H. H. Rowley describes the concept:

In early Israel man was thought of primarily as a member of a community. His individual act might involve consequences for the community. Thus Achan's sin in preserving for his own use what should have been destroyed as an offering to God brought disaster on the nation (Joshua 7). His sin might lead others into sin. (1941:145)

Provision for dealing with both individual and corporate sin was made through ritual on the Day of Atonement when the sins of the community were conceived of as transferred to the goat and sent away into the wilderness (Lev. 16:21ff.). The local church might be strengthened as a corporate group by acting on this concept. Experiencing corporateness in this way might also make it more natural to move into mission as a corporate body.

9. In many churches in the Third World "stewardship" is a problem. If the concepts concerning the relationship to spiritual powers in the society's worldview were understood, the problem might be handled very differently. For the Thai, a small amount is given at the temple or spirit house when a need is expressed; then when the request is answered, a larger amount is given. These gifts include flowers, incense, food, or other items. In the church perhaps things other than just cash should be accepted and certainly could be tied more closely to God's blessing and to personal needs. The worldview of the Westerner generally focuses on regular giving and often overlooks the special blessing time as a time when God should have more. Some churches in Nigeria take a special offering as a part of each worship service when individuals or small groups bring forward their gift to God and express to the audience what it is for, for example, the healing that week of a son or the finding of a job.

Regular giving at church for the Kamwe is often difficult because they are an agricultural people and money is scarce at certain times of the year. At harvest there is opportunity to bring to church bags of peanuts or grain to be sold, with the money used for God's work. I have also wondered if each family should together take its offering to the front and present it as one gift — in order to reinforce group responsibility, solidarity, and unity before God.

10. The church among the Kamwe, Thai, and Navajo needs to have in its structure a means of dealing with physical illness, since spiritual powers are so often perceived as the cause. This could be a regular part of worship, or it may fit the culture better to have the pastor or an elder and a prayer team available to go to homes on call, or a separate prayer team could be assigned to care for each extended family group in the church. Christians should be prepared to confront the evil powers in Jesus' name. This would affirm God's interest in the whole person and enable his name to be glorified in physical and spiritual healing. If nothing is done by the church and people are encouraged to use only the Western-style clinics and hospitals, the spiritual side of sickness is not addressed.

It might be a good idea to set aside a member of the pastoral staff whose assignment/ordination is to care for the physical and spiritual needs of the congregation. This person would be trained and gifted in healing and deliverance. In a society where there is witchcraft, sorcery, and evil spirit activity of many kinds it would be good to have a staff person available at all times. As God works through that person, it is possible that non-Christians would also be interested in assistance.

CONTEXTUALIZATION OF CHRISTIANITY

Contextualization is the process by which the people of God guided by the Holy Spirit apply the Word of God to their own life situation. Dean S. Gilliland clearly describes this process:

> Contextualized theology, therefore, is the dynamic reflection carried out by the particular church upon its own life in light of the Word of God and historic Christian truth. Guided by the Holy Spirit, the church continually challenges, incorporates, and transforms elements of the cultural milieu, bringing these under the Lordship of Christ. (1989:12)

Western theology has come into being in response to the philosophical questions of the day. Likewise, each non-Western group needs to be free to seek answers from Scripture and thereby develop a theology using its worldview as the springboard. So contextualization is an ongoing process in which the body of Christ seeks to understand and follow the Bible and its truth in its own cultural setting.

Harvie Conn refers to Third World church leaders objecting to the Western nature of their borrowed theological systems:

> Their agony is not usually so much over theology as over the construction of a logically coherent system, organized around a Western historical agenda insisted upon as universal by the Western church. They cry out for the missiological dimension to creed making. The mission of the gospel to their cultural worlds demands creedal attention to ancestor worship, polygamy, the Islamic state, to group movement conversions and how to shepherd them. (1984:222–23)

He also discusses worldview differences between middle-class theologians and the poor as they view the Bible, often with a different emphasis between theology and practice (1984:317–20). An openness and acceptance of insights from the body of Christ in a variety of places will allow for a more complete Christian Bible-based theology.

Wayne Dye explains how the worldview of a people in Papua New Guinea got in the way of understanding God's power:

> It was the presuppositions of those church leaders in the Sepik region which led them to conclude the missionaries were withholding God's power by insisting on small portions at communion. Ritual cannibalism once was fairly wide-spread, ... and the supporting ideology is still held by many of my friends there. One ate portions of someone's body to obtain some of the supernatural power he held when he was alive. The more one ate the more of this power one obtained. Jesus told the disciples to eat his body in the same discourse in which he revealed most about the coming Holy Spirit. To someone with their presupposition the conclusion is obvious. The presence and consequent power of God's Spirit comes from eating Jesus' body; the more one eats the more power. (1982:21)

Based on their worldview and history this was a natural interpretation. They had learned the gospel message of Christ's birth, life, death, and resurrection, but there was still need for a more complete study of God's power and how it is made available to his people. Careful teaching of the biblical meaning of Communion will need to be given also. This illustration shows the importance of seeing contextualization as a process dealing with questions and problems as they arise.

All Christians begin studying the Bible by looking through their own worldview lenses, but as they continue, there is gradually change in their worldview to fit better with the worldview reflected in Scripture. To illustrate, if an American who through worldview conditioning has learned to be independent and see others as a means of self-promotion becomes a follower of Christ, in time he/she will become more concerned and loving to others. But this does not mean that there will ever be complete agreement on the meaning of biblical passages. At a meeting of Africans and European missionaries, Jacob Loewen asked the main point of the story of Joseph in the Old Testament (C. Kraft 1979:9). Contrasting worldviews generated different responses: the Africans saw Joseph as one who never forgot his family, and the missionaries saw him as one who remained faithful to God.

This overview of contextualization leads us now to the main focus of this section: those areas of the process of contextualization that may be relevant to the Thai, Kamwe, and Navajo based on their worldviews, with special focus on spiritual power. I will suggest some questions that might need to be answered for them from Scripture. I recognize that I can only make suggestions; the definitive answers will come from insiders.

1. The subject of how the Christian relates to ancestor spirits needs to be faced in light of what the Bible teaches. While the Bible does not allow ancestors to be worshiped, does it allow ancestors to be shown reverence and honor? Much more work needs to be done that includes the perspective of the Third World regarding ancestors. In Korea the early Christians followed the missionary prohibition of ancestor worship, but now many years later some Korean pastors are seeking a functional substitute for the non-Christian ceremonies. Some have instituted memorial services to honor ancestors (Tippett 1987:192).

2. An emphasis needs to be placed on God's omnipotence over all other spiritual powers. He is absolute and has final say in everything. A definition of the spirit world as spelled out in the Bible, with a description of the roles of God, angels, Satan, demons/evil spirits, and the Holy Spirit, would be edifying. Serious thought and discussion on the people's own classification of spiritual powers would ensue. Witchcraft continues to be a problem in each of these societies, and the Christian needs to have a firm foundational understanding that God is more powerful than all evil powers. The church must respond biblically to the spiritual-power needs of the Christians in order to be relevant in the eyes of the society.

3. Spiritual warfare between the kingdom of God and the kingdom of Satan needs to be discussed and accepted as a reality (Matt. 12:22–29; Eph. 6:10–17). There should also be discussion of the fact that the world is in the hands of the evil one (1 John 5:19). These discussions will help put real experiences into perspective and will lead to the affirmation that God in Christ's death and resurrection is the victor.

4. The meaning of being "in Christ" needs to be understood based on Scripture. When one gives allegiance to Christ, one becomes a member of God's family. This gives a newness (2 Cor. 5:17) in identity and responsibility. God uses his power to protect his own, but he also demands loyalty and obedience from his family. Being "in Christ" also means that God has given his power to us — power over the evil spirits (Matt. 10:1; Luke 10:9). Societies oriented around spiritual power need to understand the parameters of God's power available to his own. By possessing the power of God, the believer should fear no force that is subject to God's authority. The New Testament says that God provides power so we can do his work (Mark 10:29, 40; 20:26; 1 Cor. 9:8).

5. The responsibility of human beings to the rest of creation takes on new meaning when looked at through the Navajo worldview. The relationship needs to be defined according to Scripture. Is there limited good? How much of nature's resources does the Christian have a right to? Is it a spiritual relationship?

6. The concept of blessing in the Old Testament has the basic meaning of conferring beneficial power, so a study of it would be useful. A deep

consciousness of God's concern and care for his own is seen in blessing. Greetings of blessing are found in the New Testament and should prove helpful, especially in societies that are in such close touch interpersonally and with spirit powers.

7. The Scriptures should be searched to see how God has won specific spiritual conflicts. Many power encounters are recorded (1 Samuel 5; 1 Kings 18; Dan. 10:13). When God uses one of his people to confront a spiritual power, he gives guidance in the incident. Each power encounter is a little different in the way it is carried out. The purpose of the encounter is always that God may be glorified — not humans. Such an encounter is a witness to the power of God to those who watch.

In summary, worldview beliefs related to spiritual power are important to allegiance encounter, power encounter, and truth encounter. When one declares allegiance to God instead of to the world, another spiritual power, self, or the family, worldview changes will follow. In order for persons to pledge allegiance to Christ, they must see him as relevant to real life. In societies oriented around spiritual power, God must be presented as the powerful one. Power encounters show God's relationship to other spiritual powers. When there is considerable spirit activity, conflicts and power encounters will follow. Believers are strengthened as they see God at work subduing the powers.

Truth encounter is another dimension of this. This is the dimension often in primary focus in the Western rational mind. Westerners invest much effort in knowing the truth, and rightly so. However, our cultural limitations and looking through our own worldview lenses limit our view. We can know the truth, and we know it is in the Word of God, but we cannot know all truth (1 Cor. 13:12). As I see it, Christians in each culture who strive to know God, study his Word, and follow the teaching of the Holy Spirit will find truth. But to judge what is real and what is imaginary as relates to spiritual powers, or even what is good and what is evil, must be done by the insider under the guidance of the Holy Spirit.

Chapter 12

Conclusion

Communication is measured not in what the sender sends, nor what the receptor receives, but in the correspondence between what the sender sends and the receptor receives. (Hiebert 1989:117)

This quote highlights the purpose of this book. I have worked on developing some "correspondence" between the communicator and the receptor by alerting the communicator to the importance of the worldview programming of the receptor in regard to spiritual powers. The communicator's lack of awareness of the receptor's spiritual-power needs may block the possibility of Christ and his Word serving the whole person. Failure to focus on these felt needs often causes the receptor to look elsewhere or combine religious practices in an un-Christian way.

My research has revealed a variety of common felt needs that drive human beings to seek spiritual assistance. These needs vary from the safe delivery of a baby to protection from witchcraft to cure for an illness to winning the lottery. The potential receptor of the gospel is already relating to specific spiritual powers in a prescribed way in order to meet these felt needs. The three case studies have illustrated a variety of beliefs regarding spiritual powers. I have attempted to show that the receptor's worldview should affect how the gospel is presented and the establishment of the church; it always affects how the message is heard.

I have demonstrated that if faith in Christ and the church are to meet the spiritual-power needs of a people, then missionaries must first understand the present beliefs and values held by that society. In many societies of the world many areas of life are "spiritual" that are not so to the Westerner. If these are not dealt with, problems in being faithful to God will arise. Using the case study material, I have demonstrated how to strategize for more effective Christian work.

Although differences in worldview between the communicator and the receptor affect their readings of the Bible, it still may be used to clarify the

message and guide the convert, laying a firm foundation for the body of
Christ. It is my desire that the material on how God supplied his power
to a variety of societies in biblical times will give insights, understanding, and stimulus for communicating with societies oriented around spiritual
power.

GENERAL MISSIOLOGICAL THEORY

The study of the dynamics of felt needs and spiritual power is important to missiology in both theory and practice. Worldview studies have been
done to guide in more effective communication of the gospel, but the focus
on spiritual-power needs and how worldview both reflects and shapes those
needs is a new approach. It has commonly been the assumption of missionaries that Christianity as practiced and defined to meet our felt needs will
automatically do the same in other societies. Little effort has been made to
investigate and understand why and how the receptor already reaches out for
spiritual power.

Something has been neglected when we are told by those in societies oriented on spiritual power that Christianity does not offer such power. Related
to this perception we find that even Christians in the Third World often go
to diviners and spirit doctors to have their needs for spiritual power met. Often mission effort and funding have been directed primarily into institutions.
This has tended to fog up the message of good news and has had a secularizing effect. Focusing on a personal relationship with the all-powerful God
and a readiness to adapt our programs will assist in this area. It is essential
that the gospel meet peoples' need for spiritual power and be made relevant
within their worldview. If we continue to fail in this area, syncretism will
continue to result.

The spirit world is part of God's great creation, for he created "everything
in heaven and on earth, the seen and the unseen things" (Col. 1:16). God created human beings with a need for the spiritual (Eccl. 3:11). He designed
human beings to have a personal relationship with him, to glorify him, and
to obey him. We see this demonstrated supremely in the example of Jesus'
life on earth (John 4:34). The limitations that go with being human and the
existence of something beyond combine in causing people to search for assistance when they face difficult times. Satan and evil spirits are ruling the
world (Luke 4:6; John 14:30; 1 John 5:19) and actively involved in deceit
and destruction (Luke 13:16; Acts 5:3; 1 Cor. 5:5; 2 Thess. 2:9, 10; Rev.
12:9). Since Jesus ushered in the kingdom of God, there has been tension
with the kingdom of Satan (Matt. 12:22–29). The final spiritual battle has
been won, however, in Christ's death and resurrection (Col. 2:15).

It has been my basic premise throughout this book that God is a God of power, and the gospel must carry this message clearly to societies like those in the three case studies. Jesus taught this both by word and by demonstration. As his followers, we, too, must teach God's power through word and demonstration. The Holy Spirit within us is our basic source of power, and Jesus has given us power with authority to do his work (Luke 9:1; Mark 16:15–18). Prayer and obedience to God are required in order to be ready for ministry, and then we can move out on behalf of Jesus to do his work (C. Kraft 1989:149, 174). It is always important to remember that God's power is given to be used for his purposes (see Dye 1982, as quoted on page 122).

When we realize that the real world includes evil powers and that Jesus has empowered us with his Spirit to act on his behalf and be a part of his victory over evil, we are then ready for power encounters. As these situations come up in ministry and daily living, we will be ready and able to take authority in Jesus' name and under the direction of the Holy Spirit within us and confront the evil powers.

Neither Jesus nor Paul went out looking for power encounters, nor should we. However, when we are confronted with a potential power encounter, we must not let Satan and evil powers win. We must, rather, take authority as Jesus did and defeat the enemy. This will speak clearly to those in spiritual-power–oriented societies. Since demonstrating God's power is for his purposes, the same approach should be taken in praying for the sick. The initiative should be taken by those who seek us out or by God showing us through prayer that he wants us to go to that specific sick person.

Through teaching and modeling both the missionary and the local pastor will be presenting a clearer message of the true gospel. At times it is easier for the local pastor as an insider with the help of intuition and knowledge of the worldview of the people to step out in faith and claim God's authority and power over sickness and evil spirits.

GENERAL MISSIOLOGICAL APPLICATION

By focusing on the Navajo, the Thai, and the Kamwe, I have illustrated throughout the book how worldview and felt needs affect the presentation of the gospel and the establishing of the church. I firmly believe that God accepts us where he finds us and gives salvation. Then he begins gently reshaping our lives, a process that will involve worldview changes. He is patient, and as we positively focus on God and study his Word, our values, priorities, and even our assumptions eventually change.

For the Outside Advocate

When the current spiritual-power beliefs in the receptor's worldview are understood, we can search out the necessary Scripture passages to develop credibility for Christianity and for us as Christ's representatives. We also will be able to see in a positive way the preparation that God has made already in that society for the gospel, such as dependence on spiritual resources for daily needs and values much like those taught in the Bible for interpersonal relationships.

Understanding how the receptors are programmed for interaction with spiritual powers will give helpful insight for establishing the church. Recognizing perceived dangers in life caused by spirit beings allows us to prepare a biblical and Christian response. It has not been successful in the past to try to convince the receptors that those dangers do not exist. If sickness and misfortune are perceived to be caused by witchcraft or spirit attack, we must be able to deal with them on a spiritual level, knowing God is more powerful. It is important to know how we can work with God in that power. Liturgy and ceremonies, both in and out of the church, may be needed to regularly affirm the power of the God we serve.

Mission organizations must realize the dangers involved in "transplanting" the church from one society to another. The theological abstractions of the West often have very little relevance to life as people of other societies experience it. It is far better to carefully define the church and what it means to accept Christ from a scriptural base, and then let believers develop and grow as a church through God's Word and Spirit. They will find answers to their needs from the Bible, and in this way their spiritual-power needs will also be dealt with.

For the Inside Advocate

The local church has the responsibility to equip believers for living in the world around them as well as to reach out to those who are not Christian. When the activity of evil spirits is a part of the local reality, Christians must be trained in how to deal with them. The present forms and structures in the church should be reevaluated to see if the spiritual-power needs of the believers are being dealt with in terms of the truths of the gospel. Some of the topics that may need specific Bible teaching are the following: how to protect oneself from curses and evil power attacks, the role of the Holy Spirit as it relates to spiritual power, how to confront spiritual powers as a Christian, spirit possession and deliverance, Christ's victory over the evil powers, God's attitude toward soothsayers, magic, and amulets.

Local church leaders need to determine how spiritual-power needs can be met through the church. Some rituals will be needed, raising questions such as: What rituals are needed? What should the setting be — church, home, public, private? Should the form be an addition to an already existing ritual? What group should meet together for this purpose? At what time of day? What Scripture should be used? Is group prayer or individual prayer best in this situation? What symbolism is suitable? Would it be good for non-Christians to witness this ritual?

Specific Scriptures for arming Christians for spiritual warfare could profitably be memorized and recited as a part of worship. Passages that show God's faithfulness and protection of his people need to be taught and maybe even dramatized or put into song so they will be more easily remembered. A key idea from Scripture that is illustrated over and over is that God uses his power to accomplish his purposes, and human beings are God's agents in the action. A time of sharing what God is doing can be incorporated into the church format. This will reinforce appreciation of and experience with the powerful God that we serve. Meeting people's needs is more important than many of the church traditions.

For Training Workers

At present there is need for special training for Christian workers, both Western and non-Western, because of the lack of focusing on spiritual warfare in seminaries and Bible schools. This is an area where theological training definitely reflects Western blindspots. Activity by evil spirits is found in all but one of the books of the New Testament, yet very little attention is given in seminary and Bible school curricula to evil spirits and the power they wield. Training can be done through spiritual-power or spiritual-warfare seminars or by apprenticing, working with someone who has a ministry focusing on spiritual power. Hands-on experience is always useful in processing new material.

Mission organizations from the West and from the national church need to train workers in the importance of learning from the receptor as well as from Scripture. Several specific suggestions for using the existing worldview as a starting point for the communication of Christ are as follows:

1. Be a learner of the basic assumptions and values of the receptors/ non-Christians. Look for their religious beliefs and see how they fulfill spiritual-power needs. What artifacts in the culture represent spiritual power? What fears of spirit powers exist and how are they handled? Is the perceived cause for misfortune and illness ever or always spiritual power? When are the specific stress times in which beyond-human power is needed?

2. Begin to recognize the great variety of spiritual-power needs God can meet. Western society has not given God a chance in many cases because hu-

mans have taken over in so many areas. Begin to visualize God in roles you have not before considered — as the one who sends rain when it is needed, as the healer, as the giver of the harvest crop, as the provider of wisdom when it is needed, as the mender of broken relationships.

3. Begin to search the Word of God for insights and answers to the spiritual-power needs you see around you. Seek the guidance of the Holy Spirit in teaching you.

4. Be ready to learn from the local believers by taking the role of learner and friend. Often they see things in better perspective because they know the non-Christian setting. Be ready to learn from "new" believers. Their response to the life of Christ and teaching from the Bible may give you new insights. Answers to their problems may come easier to them because their culture is more like biblical cultures. Constantly remind yourself that you see things through your worldview lenses and that your walk with God strongly reflects your worldview conditioning.

One of the things my research has shown is how easy it is for Christians, in forming a strong group striving to become more Christlike, to get out of touch with what is going on in the life of non-Christians. Because the church is intended by God to spread the gospel and make disciples, it is significant to know the potential receptors of his message. Their spiritual beliefs and practices and the functions they serve should be part of the training given church workers. Sometimes modernization causes both spiritual beliefs and practices to go underground. Christians and their leaders often become ghettoized and assume that everything has changed. Practitioners in spiritual power, however, work quietly but faithfully to serve the people. When backed into a corner with no other answers for a problem, many people — even those who have gone to school and changed many of their ideas about life — will seek out the traditional practitioner for assistance. Spiritual-power needs may also be met by or intensified by the presence of other powerful practitioners in the society. This is the case among the Kamwe with the Muslim teachers in the towns. These Muslim priests are heavily into sorcery and curses as well as cures and providing amulets. Christian workers need to be in touch with the total scene of spiritual power in order to be most effective and relevant in doing God's work.

THE IMPACT OF MODERNIZATION

As has been discussed in chapter 9, tradition forms the basis for the modernizing process. The worldview of the society affects the areas where modernization is allowed and the extent to which change is accepted. We cannot assume that modernization makes people "like us." Often, for example, those who represent modernization in another land speak another language, are deeply tied to an extended family, readily share their income with relatives, and have parental arrangement as the dominant mode of marital selection.

Worldview changes do not come as quickly as surface-level changes within a society. For instance, a worldview that sees spiritual causes of sickness will rarely be fully or easily displaced by a worldview that emphasizes Western medicine. It is more common to find Western medicine used for some kinds of sicknesses and "spiritual" treatment for others. Or sometimes the response is the need for both Western medicine and "spiritual" treatment in order to be restored to health. Or perhaps one is tried after the other to see which works in a given situation.

In the modernization process things often move so fast in adjusting to changes in the material environment and through the addition of new technology that the spiritual aspect is neglected. To illustrate, when the family becomes scattered due to schooling and work, in a society where the ancestors heavily influenced the morals of the society, ancestor spirit power often can no longer control the moral behavior of the youth. The new environment, new rules for living, and distance from the traditional controls result in new problems. With the Kamwe a girl who has gotten pregnant before marriage is not desired for marriage. Because modernization tends to increase the number of premarital pregnancies, this complex problem has become more frequent.

The church must be constantly alert to the ills of society that come with the modernization process. Especially since many of the adjustments involve spirit-world concepts, the church must be ready to analyze the situation, seek God's guidance, and be a leader in dealing with problems. The one just mentioned may necessitate special Bible teaching for the young people, showing their responsibility to God; Christian youth organizations may need to encourage and assist the young women in their extended time of being alone and may need to offer specific help in understanding the dangers and consequences of immoral behavior.

In the Kamwe system the Creator God was perceived as far away, and the ancestor spirits were close and active. With the involvement and control of ancestor spirits beginning to break down, Christians must experience a holistic relationship to Christ, recognizing his covenant and closeness and what this implies for behavior. The tendency of the church has been to rely on human rules and regulations reinforced through sermons. This is not working. The church seems to have started in the Spirit and turned to the flesh (Gal. 3:3). It seems like moral standards once enforced by spiritual power need now to be enforced by different spiritual power. Personal relationship to Christ and awareness of his love and indwelling presence as well as commitment of the whole self should provide a spiritual solution to the problem. What was under accountability to the ancestors can comfortably be under personal accountability to Christ.

Modernization brings new dangers and fears and often a turn to obtaining spiritual power for these needs. The increased number of mediums in the cities of Thailand is evidence of this. The church needs to investigate what in the modernization process drives people to seek spiritual assistance and then adapt its program so that Christians will seek Christ for this assistance. To illustrate, often the traditional rules for marriage begin to break down. Should the parents of the bride allow her to go live with the groom's people as they are insisting, or should they hold out for the traditional where the groom joins the bride's family (as in Thailand)? The church must develop a reputation of dealing with practical problems such as these and have available counselors trained to deal with both physical and spiritual dimensions for a Christian solution.

For today's world solid courses in spiritual warfare based on the research of local worldview of spiritual power and biblical teaching should be part of current seminary and Bible-school training. Questions such as the following need to be investigated: How does the change of allegiance to Christ influence the worldview? What areas are changed and how is this change brought about? How can faith in Christ focus primarily on worldview change and not on policing new behavior? How important are power encounters to worldview change? These are exciting days to be on the front lines for Christ and his kingdom.

References Cited

Aberle, David F.
  1982   *The Peyote Religion among the Navaho.* 2d ed. Chicago: University of Chicago Press.

Adair, John, and Kert Deuschle
  1970   *The People's Health: Medicine and Anthropology in a Navajo Community.* New York: Meredith Corporation.

Adams, Richard N.
  1974   "Harnessing Technological Development." In *Rethinking Modernization: Anthropological Perspectives*, ed. John J. Poggie, Jr., and Robert Lynch, 37–68. Westport, Conn.: Greenwood Press.

Arnold, Clinton E.
  1989   *Ephesians, Power and Magic: The Concept of Power in Ephesians in Light of Its Historical Setting.* New York: Cambridge University Press.
  1992   *Powers of Darkness: Principalities and Powers in Paul's Letters.* Downers Grove, Ill.: InterVarsity Press.

Barnett, Homer G.
  1953   *Innovation: The Basis of Cultural Change.* New York: McGraw-Hill.

Barrett, David B., ed.
  1982   *World Christian Encyclopedia.* New York: Oxford University Press.

Bazza, Margaret
  1990   Personal interview.

Bellah, Robert N., et al.
  1986   *Habits of the Heart: Individualism and Commitment in American Life.* New York: Harper and Row.

Berger, Peter L.
  1977   *Facing Up to Modernity.* New York: Basic Books.

Berger, Peter L., Brigitte Berger, and Hansfried Kellner
  1973   *The Homeless Mind: Modernization and Consciousness.* New York: Random House.

Berkhof, Hendrikus
  1962   *Christ and the Powers.* Trans. John Howard Yoder. Scottdale, Pa.: Herald Press.

Caird, G. B.
1956 *Principalities and Powers.* Oxford: Clarendon Press.

Chance, Norman A.
1974 "Modernization and Educational Reform in Native Alaska." In *Rethinking Modernization: Anthropological Perspectives,* ed. John J. Poggie, Jr., and Robert Lynch, 332–52. Westport, Conn.: Greenwood Press.

Codrington, R. H.
1891 *The Melanesians.* Oxford: Clarendon Press.

Conn, Harvie M.
1984 *Eternal Word and Changing Worlds: Theology, Anthropology, and Mission in Trialogue.* Grand Rapids: Academic Books.

Dolaghan, Thomas, and David Scates
1978 *The Navajos Are Coming to Jesus.* Pasadena: William Carey Library.

DomNwachukwu, Chinaka S.
1990 *Demons Are Real.* Lagos, Nigeria: Integrated Press.

Donovan, Vincent J.
1982 *Christianity Rediscovered.* Maryknoll, N.Y.: Orbis Books.

Downs, James F.
1972 *The Navajo.* New York: Holt, Rinehart and Winston.

Dye, Wayne
1982 "Toward a Theology of Power for Melanesia." Paper, School of World Mission, Fuller Theological Seminary, Pasadena.

Evers, Hans-Dieter
1973 "Group Conflict and Class Formation in South-East Asia." In *Modernization in South-East Asia,* ed. Hans-Dieter Evers, 110–32. London: Oxford University Press.

Filson, Floyd V.
1950 *The New Testament against Its Environment.* London: SCM Press Ltd.

Fison, Lorimer
1892 "The President's Address." In *The Proceedings of the Australasian Association for the Advancement of Science,* Anthropological Section, 144–53. Hobart, Australia.

Fohrer, Georg
1972 *History of Israelite Religion.* Trans. David E. Green. Nashville: Abingdon Press.

Garrett, Susan R.
1989 *The Demise of the Devil: Magic and the Demonic in Luke's Writings.* Minneapolis: Fortress Press.

Gilliland, Dean S., ed.
1989 *The Word among Us.* Dallas: Word.

Gorman, Carl
   1974   "The Energy of All Life." In the *Navajo Times,* March 7 and 14, 1974.

Guillaume, Alfred
   1938   *Prophecy and Divination among the Hebrews and Other Semites.* London: Hodder and Stoughton.

Guli, John
   1990   Personal interview.

Gusfield, Joseph R.
   1967   "Tradition and Modernity: Misplaced Polarities in the Study of Social Change." *American Journal of Sociology* 72:351–62.

Gustafson, James
   1970   "Syncretistic Rural Thai Buddhism." M.A. thesis, School of World Mission, Fuller Theological Seminary, Pasadena.

Hackett, Rosalind J.
   1985   "Sacred Paradoxes: Women and Religious Plurality in Nigeria." In *Women, Religion, and Social Change,* ed. Yvonne Yazbeck Haddad and Ellison Banks Findley, 247–71. Albany: State University of New York Press.

Haddad, Yvonne Yazbeck, and Ellison Banks Findley, eds.
   1985   *Women, Religion, and Social Change.* Albany: State University of New York Press.

Herskovits, Melville S.
   1951   *Man and His Works.* New York: Alfred A. Knopf.
   1962   *The Human Factor in Changing Africa.* New York: Alfred A. Knopf.

Hiebert, Paul G.
   1976   *Cultural Anthropology.* Grand Rapids: Baker Book House.
   1982   "The Flaw of the Excluded Middle." *Missiology* 10:35–47.
   1985   *Anthropological Insights for Missionaries.* Grand Rapids: Baker Book House.
   1989   "Form and Meaning in Contextualization of the Gospel." In *The Word among Us,* ed. Dean S. Gilliland, 101–20. Dallas: Word.

Hill, Evelyn
   1985   Personal Interview.

Hughes, Philip
   1982   "Christianity and Culture: A Case Study in Northern Thailand." Ph.D. diss., South East Asia Graduate School of Theology.

Jilek, Wolfgang, and Louise Jilek-Aall
   1981   "The Psychiatrist and His Shaman Colleague." In *Human Services for Cultural Minorities,* ed. R. H. Dana. Baltimore: University Press.

Junod, Henri A.
   1962   *The Life of a South African Tribe.* 2 vols. Reprint, New York: University Books.

Keyes, Charles F.
  1977   *The Golden Peninsula: Culture and Adaptation in Mainland Southeast
          Asia.* New York: Macmillan.

Kopf, David
  1982   "Modernization and Westernization: Process and Patterning in History." In
          Tradition and Modernity, ed. Jessie G. Lutz and Selah El-Shakhs, 7–21.
          Washington, D.C.: University Press of America.

Kraft, Charles H.
  1963   "Christian Conversion or Cultural Conversion?" *Practical Anthropology*
          10:179–87.
  1976   "Cultural Concomitants of Higi Conversion: Early Period." *Missiology*
          4:431–42.
  1979   *Christianity in Culture.* Maryknoll, N.Y.: Orbis Books.
  1989   *Christianity with Power: Your Worldview and Your Experience of the
          Supernatural.* Ann Arbor: Vine Books.
  1991a   *Communication Theory for Christian Witness.* Nashville: Abingdon Press.
  1991b   "What Kind of Encounters Do We Need in Our Christian Witness?"
          Evangelical Missions Quarterly 27:258–65.

Kraft, Marguerite G.
  1978   *Worldview and the Communication of the Gospel: A Nigerian Case Study.*
          Pasadena: William Carey Library.
  1990   "Reaching Out for Spiritual Power: A Study in the Dynamics of Felt
          Needs and Spiritual Power." Ph.D. diss. School of World Mission, Fuller
          Theological Seminary, Pasadena.

Lambo, T. Adeoye
  1964   "Patterns of Psychiatric Care in Developing African Countries." In *Magic,
          Faith and Healing,* ed. Ari Kiev, 443–53. New York: Free Press.

LaSor, William S.
  1984   "Zoroastrianism." In *Evangelical Dictionary of Theology,* ed. Walter A.
          Elwell, 1202. Grand Rapids: Baker Book House.

Linton, Ralph
  1940   "The Distinctive Aspects of Acculturation." In *Acculturation in Seven
          American Indian Tribes,* ed. Ralph Linton. New York: D. Appleton. Re-
          printed in *The Emergent Native Americans: A Reader in Culture Contact,*
          ed. D. E. Walker, 6–19. Boston: Little, Brown and Company, 1972.
  1952   "Universal Ethical Principles: An Anthropological View." In *Moral Prin-
          ciples of Action: Man's Ethical Imperative,* ed. Ruth Nanda Anshen. New
          York: Harper and Brothers.

Luzbetak, Louis J.
  1988   *The Church and Cultures: New Perspectives in Missiological Anthropology.*
          Maryknoll, N.Y.: Orbis Books.

Malinowski, Bronislaw
  1931   "Primitive Religion and Primitive Science." In Julian Huxley et al., *Science
          and Religion: A Symposium.* London: Gerald Howe.

Mandelbaum, David G., ed.
　1958　*Selected Writings of Edward Sapir in Language, Culture, and Personality.* Berkeley: University of California Press.

Marett, R. R.
　1929　*The Threshold of Religion.* London: Methuen.

Marris, Peter
　1962　*Family and Social Change in an African City.* Evanston, Ill.: Northwestern University Press.

Maslow, Abraham H.
　1970　*Motivation and Personality.* New York: Harper and Row.

Mbiti, John S.
　1976　"Theological Impotence and the Universality of the Church." In *Mission Trends Number 3: Third World Theologies,* ed. Gerald H. Anderson and Thomas F. Stransky, 6–18. Grand Rapids: Wm. B. Eerdmans Publishing Co. (original, *Lutheran World* 21, no. 3 [1974]).

Mead, Margaret
　1974　"Changing Perspectives on Modernization." In *Rethinking Modernization: Anthropological Perspectives,* ed. John J. Poggie, Jr., and Robert Lynch, 21–36. Westport, Conn.: Greenwood Press.

Meek, C. K.
　1931　*Tribal Studies in Northern Nigeria.* Vol. I. London: Kegan, Paul, Trench, Tribner and Co.

Navajo Times
　1974　Vol. 15., no. 40.

Newbigin, Lesslie
　1966　*Honest Religion for Secular Man.* Philadelphia: Westminster Press.

Newport, John
　1976　"Satan and Demons: A Theological Perspective." In *Demon Possession,* ed. J. W. Montgomery, 325–45. Minneapolis: Bethany Fellowship.

Opler, Morris E.
　1946　"Themes as Dynamic Forces in Culture." *American Journal of Sociology* 51:198–206.

Parrinder, Geoffrey
　1954　*African Traditional Religion.* New York: Hutchinson's University Library.
　1969　*Religion in Africa.* New York: Praeger.

Phillips, Herbert P.
　1966　*Thai Peasant Personality: The Patterning of Interpersonal Behavior in the Village of Bang Chan.* Los Angeles: University of California Press.

Poggie, John J., Jr., and Robert Lynch, eds.
　1974　*Rethinking Modernization: Anthropological Perspectives.* Westport, Conn.: Greenwood Press.

Potter, Sulamith Heins
　　1977　　*Family Life in a Northern Thai Village: A Study in the Structural Significance of Women.* Los Angeles: University of California Press.

Rajadhon, Phya Anuman
　　1968　　*Essays on Thai Folklore.* Bangkok: Editions Duang Kamol.

Ranger, Albert
　　1986　　Personal interview.

Redfield, Robert
　　1953　　*The Primitive World and Its Transformations.* Ithaca, N.Y.: Cornell University Press.

Reichard, Gladys A.
　　1944　　*Prayer: The Compulsive Word.* Seattle: University of Washington Press.

Ringgren, Helmer
　　1966　　*Israelite Religion.* Trans. David E. Green. Philadelphia: Fortress Press.

Rogers, Everett
　　1969　　*Modernization among Peasants: The Impact of Communication.* New York: Holt, Rinehart and Winston.

Rowley, H. H.
　　1941　　*The Relevance of the Bible.* London: James Clarke.

Russell, Jeffrey Burton
　　1977　　*The Devil: Perceptions of Evil from Antiquity to Primitive Christianity.* Ithaca, N.Y.: Cornell University Press.
　　1981　　*Satan: The Early Christian Tradition.* Ithaca, N.Y.: Cornell University Press.
　　1984　　*Lucifer: The Devil in the Middle Ages.* Ithaca, N.Y.: Cornell University Press.
　　1986　　*Mephistopheles: The Devil in the Modern World.* Ithaca, N.Y.: Cornell University Press.
　　1988　　*The Prince of Darkness: Radical Evil and the Power of Good in History.* Ithaca, N.Y.: Cornell University Press.

Saowkaweow, Bon
　　1985　　Personal interview.

Sapir, Edward
　　1927　　"The Unconscious Patterning of Behavior in Society." Reprinted in *Selected Writings of Edward Sapir in Language, Culture, and Personality,* ed. David G. Mandelbaum. Berkeley: University of California Press, 1958.
　　1929　　"The Status of Linguistics as a Science." *Language* 5:207–14.

Scates, David
　　1981　　*Why Navajo Churches Are Growing.* Grand Junction, Colo.: Navajo Christian Churches.

Schlier, Heinrich
    1961   *Principalities and Powers in the New Testament.* Edinburgh-London:
            Nelson.

Shipp, Horace
    1946   *Faiths That Moved the World.* London: Evans Brothers.

Singer, Milton
    1966   "The Modernization of Religious Beliefs." In *Modernization: The Dynam-
            ics of Growth,* ed. Myron Weiner, 55–67. New York: Basic Books.

Smith, Edwin
    1923   *The Religion of Lower Races: As Illustrated by the African Bantu.* New
            York: Macmillan.
    1950   *African Ideas of God.* London: Edinburgh House.

Snaith, Norman H.
    1957   "The Authority of the Bible." In *Ninth World Methodist Conference,* ed.
            E. T. Clark and E. B. Perkins, 122–30. Nashville: Methodist Publishing
            House.

Songkham, Boon Thaen
    1985   Personal interview.

Subinraht, Khamai
    1985   Personal Interview.

Suksamran, Somboon
    1977   *Political Buddhism in Southeast Asia: The Role of the Sangha in the
            Modernization of Thailand.* Ed. Trevor O. Ling. London: C. Hurst.

Swanson, Herbert
    1984   *Khrischak Muang Nua: A Study in Northern Thai Church History.* Bang-
            kok: Chuan Printing Press.

Taeng, Mae
    1985   Personal interview.

Takwale, Joseph
    1967   "Higi Ethnography." Manuscript, School of World Mission, Fuller Theo-
            logical Seminary, Pasadena.

Taru, Iyasco
    1990   Personal interview.

Tat, Huai
    1985   Personal interview.

Taylor, John V.
    1963   *The Primal Vision.* Philadelphia: Fortress Press.

Tempels, Placide
    1945   *Bantu Philosophy.* Paris: Presence Africaine.

Tippett, Alan R.
  1967   *Solomon Islands Christianity.* London: Lutterworth Press.
  1973   *Verdict Theology in Missionary Theory.* Pasadena: William Carey Library.
  1987   *Introduction to Missiology.* Pasadena: William Carey Library.

Underhill, Ruth M.
  1956   *The Navajos.* Norman: University of Oklahoma Press.

Van Gennep, Arnold
  1960   *The Rites of Passage.* Trans. M. B. Vizedom and G. L. Coffee. Reprint, Chicago: University of Chicago Press.

Vogt, Evon Z.
  1951   *Navaho Veterans: A Study of Changing Values.* Papers of the Peabody Museum of American Archaeology, vol. 41, no. 1. Cambridge, Mass.: Peabody Museum of American Archaeology.

Westermann, D.
  1937   *Africa and Christianity.* London: Oxford University Press.

Whitehead, Henry
  1921   *The Village Gods of South India.* London: Oxford University Press.

Willard, Dallas
  1988   *The Spirit of the Disciplines.* San Francisco: Harper and Row.

Wink, Walter
  1984   *Naming the Powers: The Language of Power in the New Testament.* Philadelphia: Fortress Press.
  1986   *Unmasking the Powers: The Invisible Forces That Determine Human Existence.* Philadelphia: Fortress Press.
  1992   *Engaging the Powers: Discernment and Resistance in a World of Domination.* Minneapolis: Fortress Press.

Witherspoon, Gary
  1977   *Language and Art in the Navajo Universe.* Ann Arbor: University of Michigan Press.

Wright, G. Ernest
  1952   *God Who Acts: Biblical Theology as Recital.* London: SCM Press.
  1960   *Biblical Archeology.* Abridged ed. Philadelphia: Westminster Press.

Index

Adair, John, 98
Adams, Richard N., 92
African independent churches, 117–18
amulets
in Africa, 14
the Kamwes' use of, 106
the Navajos' use of, 75, 100
the Thais' use of, 18, 76, 104
animism, 70–71
Anselm, 46
Arnold, Clinton E., 41, 44, 60
Athanasius, 45

Bantu, the, 9
Barnett, Homer G., 92–93
barrenness: various cultures' cures for, 14–15
Berger, Brigitte, 89, 90
Berger, Peter L., 89, 90
Berkhof, Hendrikus, 41
Bible, the
contextualization and, 122–24
mission and, 114–15
New Testament on spiritual powers, 60–62
Old Testament on spiritual powers, 52–60
overview of attitude toward spiritual power in, 50–52, 62–63
and shaping local churches, 118
Brahmanism, 71
Buddhism
modernization in Thailand and, 103–4
Thai moral system and, 70–71
Thai worldview and, 76

Chance, Norman, 7–8
charismatic movements, 33
Codrington, R. H., 24–25

Conn, Harvie, 121
contextualization, 121–24

Dante, 46
Deuschle, Kert, 98
devil, the
defined, 40
See also evil spirits; Satan
Donovan, Vincent, 33
Downs, James F., 101
dualism, 79
Dye, Wayne, 114, 122

Eastern religions: Westerners and, x, 8, 33, 39
Enlightenment, the, 31
evil
defined, 39–40
human nature and, 48–49
overview of rule of, 62–63
Paul on, 41–42
See also evil spirits; powers, the
evil spirits
in Christian tradition, 44–48
the Kamwe and, 77
the Navajo and, 74
the Thais and, 76
exile, the, 59–60
exodus, the, 54–55
exorcism, 44–45, 47

Fison, Lorimer, 20
Fohrer, Georg, 59
funerals, 15–16, 106

Garrett, Susan, 41
Gilliland, Dean S., 121
Gorman, Carl, 100
Guillaume, Alfred, 53
Gusfield, Joseph, 93–94
Gustafson, James, 70

Hackett, Rosalind, 117, 118
healing
　the Kamwes' methods of, 106
　Navajo rituals for, 98
　shaping local churches' attitude
　　toward, 120–21
　the Thais' methods of, 103
　various cultures' attitudes toward,
　　16
Hiebert, Paul G., 21, 35, 90
Holy Spirit, the
　evil spirits and, 61
　magic and, 85
Hughes, Philip, 9, 104

Igbo, the, 35
Ignatius of Loyola, 47
illness. *See* healing
individualism, 23, 32–33
Islam, 40
Israelites: God's acts of power and,
　52–60

Jesus
　evil spirits and, 61–62
　miracles of, 85
　Navajo witchcraft and, 4–5
　Satan and, 41
　the spirits and, 10
Justin Martyr, 44

Kamwe, the
　classification of spiritual powers
　　among, 80
　communication of the gospel to,
　　112, 113
　history of, 71–73
　mission and, 114
　other cultures' worldviews compared
　　with, 73–74
　person-group relations among, 81
　shaping local churches among, 116,
　　117, 119, 120
　spiritual power and the worldview
　　of, 77–78
　and spiritual powers in modern
　　times, 104–6
　time-space perceptions among, 83
　view of causality, 82

karma, 71, 102
Kellner, Hansfried, 89, 90
Keyes, Charles, 102
kingdom of God, the, 61, 62
Kopf, David, 89
Kraft, Charles, 21

Lambo, T. Adeoye, 95–96
LaSor, William, 40
Lewis, C. S., 48
Linton, Ralph, 93
local churches: mission and, 115–21
Loewen, Jacob, 122
Luther, Martin, 46
Lynch, Robert, 89

magic
　in the Hellenistic world, 44, 60
　the Holy Spirit and, 85
　Paul and, 41
Malinowski, Bronislaw, 13
materialism, 26, 27
Mazdaism, 40
Mbiti, John S., 35
Mead, Margaret, 92
medicine. *See* healing
Meek, C. K., 72
Melanesians, 24–25, 29–30
merit
　Buddhist ideology of, 71, 102
　Thai worldview on, 76
Milton, John, 47
miracles, 85
mission
　contextualization of Christianity
　　and, 121–24
　general principles regarding, 127–
　　30
　general theory of, 126–27
　initial communication of the gospel
　　and, 111–13
　modernization and, 130–32
　as promoting Western values, 6
　receptor's individual growth and,
　　113–15
　and shaping the local church to meet
　　felt needs, 115–21

modernization
  concepts of spiritual power and,
    94–96
  effects on the Kamwe view of
    spiritual powers, 104–6
  effects on the Navajo view of
    spiritual powers, 97–101
  effects on the Thai view of spiritual
    powers, 102–4
  essential characteristics of, 88–91
  mission and, 130–32
  problems with, 7–8
  traditional societies and, 91–94

Native American Church. *See*
  Peyotism
nature, 31–32
Navajo, the
  classification of spiritual powers
    among, 80
  communication of the gospel to,
    112–13
  history of, 68–69
  other cultures' worldviews compared
    with, 73–74
  person-group relations among, 81
  shaping local churches among,
    116–17, 119, 120
  spiritual powers and the worldview
    of, 12, 74–75
  and spiritual powers in modern
    times, 97–101
  time-space perceptions among, 82
  view of causality, 82
  witchcraft and, 4–5
needs
  types of, 12–13, 14–19
  worldview, reality, and, 25–27
New Age religions, x, 8, 33, 39
Newbigin, Lesslie, 5
Newport, John, 34
New Testament: acts of God's power
  in, 60–62
nominalism, 46

Old Testament, the: acts of God's
  power in, 52–60
Oppler, Morris, 79

Parrinder, Geoffrey, 25
Paul: on evil, 41–42
Pentecost, 61
Pentecostalism, 33
Peyotism
  history of, 69
  overview of, 99–100
  traditional religion and, 98
Poggie, John J., Jr., 89
Potter, Sulamith Heins, 16
powers, the, 41–44

Rajadhon, Phya Anuman, 70
rationalism, x, 31
Redfield, Robert, 21
reincarnation, 71
restitution, 17–18
Rogers, Everett, 88, 89
Rowley, H. H., 119–20
Russell, Jeffrey Burton, 39–40,
  43–44, 47, 48

Sapir, Edward, 20
Satan
  in Christian tradition, 44–48
  human nature and, 48–49
  Jesus and, 61–62
  in Judaism and the early church,
    40–41
  New Testament view of, 60–61
  overview of rule of, 62–63
  Walter Wink on, 43
  See also evil spirits
Schlier, Heinrich, 41
scholasticism, 46
science
  dethronement of God by, 8
  disillusionment with, x
  Western worldview and, 26, 27,
    31
secularization, 5–6
security, 16–17, 23
sin, 119–20
Singer, Milton, 94
Smith, Edwin W., 14
Snaith, Norman, 56
specialization, 31

supernaturalism: methods of analyzing,
    79–87
syncretism, 115

Takwale, Joseph, 77
Taylor, John V., 81
technology
    effects of, on non-Western cultures,
        88
    effects of, on work, 91
    the spiritual world and, 4
    traditional cultures and, 95
Thai, the
    classification of spiritual powers
        among, 80
    communication of the gospel to, 112
    history of, 70–71
    mission and, 114
    other cultures' worldviews compared
        with, 73–74
    person-group relations among, 81
    shaping local churches among, 116,
        118, 119, 120
    spiritual power and the worldview
        of, 75–76
    and spiritual powers in modern
        times, 102–4
    time-space perceptions among,
        82–83
    view of causality, 82

Third Wave of the Holy Spirit, the, 33
Tippett, Alan R., 29–30, 115–16, 118

Underhill, Ruth, 69

Vogt, Evon, 101

Westermann, D., 14
Willard, Dallas, 5
Wink, Walter, 42–44, 49
witchcraft
    among the Navajos, 4–5, 75
    in the West, 46–47
women: local churches in Africa and,
        117–18
worldview
    changes in, 22–23
    defining, 20–22
    difficulties of Western, 34–36
    enslavement by Western, 33–34
    felt needs, reality, and, 25–27
    the Navajos', 12
    overview of the Western, 31–33
    spiritual power and, 23–25
    in spiritual-power–oriented societies,
        28–30
    universals of, 80–83
Wright, G. Ernest, 51

Zoroastrianism, 40